What Writers Need to Know About Publishing

by
Jerry D. Simmons

www.WritersReaders.com

www.NothingBinding.com

WHAT WRITERS NEED TO KNOW ABOUT PUBLISHING.

Bulk sales are available for educational purposes.
For information please visit www.WritersReaders.com and e-mail Jerry@writersreaders.com .

FIRST EDITION, available online at www.WritersReaders.com.

Library of Congress Control Number 2006907641.

ISBN 13
978-0-9789247-0-6

ISBN 10
0-9789247-0-3

Published by www.WritersReaders.com, also available through www.NothingBinding.com .

To writers,

May you forever remain true

to your craft long after you become authors.

Acknowledgement

First to my family, Lea Ann, Jared and Regan who provided unwavering support and understanding through all those nights and weekends away from home over twenty-five years. To my editor, a godsend, Nancy McCurry, where would I be without your help and encouragement? Your expertise and guidance were invaluable; I am indebted to you. To the core group of writers around the world who have encouraged me, supported me, and urged me to continue from the beginning, this book would not have been possible without you, many thanks.

CONTENTS

INTRODUCTION

Publishing should be about writers and their books. However, the competitive nature of the industry—combined with the ever-changing opportunities involved in getting a manuscript published—makes it imperative writers understand the basics and the power of the business of book publishing. The creation of this book and its accompanying website *WritersReaders.com* was conceived and developed for one simple purpose: to help writers make informed decisions. Whether you want to self-publish, get your book published by a small, traditional publisher, or land a contract with a major trade house, this book is for you. My goal is to share essential information that can—and most certainly will—have a huge effect on your career. By providing valuable inside information, this book will serve to improve your chance at achieving the ultimate goal: to become a successfully published author.

I have a tremendous amount of respect and admiration for writers whose talent and command of language identify them as the most creative in the world. Listening to these writers describe how they write and the inspirations for their work made for interesting discussion during book tours around the country.

Over the years I have been fortunate to have worked on books written by such best-selling authors as Sandra Brown, Scott Turow, Nelson DeMille, Michael Connelly, Nicholas Sparks, Alice Sebold, David Baldacci and James Patterson, to name but a few. I have also been involved with such multi-million copy bestsellers as *Bridges of Madison County, Scarlett, Simple Abundance* and *Lovely Bones,* as well as one of the longest running bestsellers in publishing history, *Rich Dad, Poor Dad.* Our sales group launched the mass market paperback edition of *Presumed Innocent,* the first blockbuster legal thriller. I've helped to market and sell such books as *Absolute Power, Along Came a Spider, Kiss the Girls* and *The Notebook,* all of which became major motion pictures. I have watched the classics *To Kill a Mockingbird* and *The Catcher in the Rye* sell hundreds of thousands of copies and I was honored to be part of the team that assisted Disney in the marketing of *The Lion King.*

Helping writers turn their stories into successfully published books was one of the most rewarding parts of my career as a sales representative In New York. Now it is my turn to give something back to those who made my more than twenty-five years in the business an enjoyable experience.

Publishing at the major trade level has become a production process for the printed word. Publishers no longer take great care of authors and their books or offer the author every opportunity to succeed in the marketplace. That kind of support has all but vanished and the reality is that most writers don't realize what lies ahead once the contract has been signed. Simply put, the process of taking a manuscript from contract to published book can be a difficult obstacle course to maneuver unless you have the right information.

Working within the publishing industry has given me firsthand experience in how books are published, sold, marketed and distributed. I can recognize the pitfalls from a publisher's perspective—pitfalls authors unknowingly face. Most importantly, I understand the industry as a whole and know your dream of becoming a published author can be damaged by the business of publishing—unless you have the right information at the right time in your journey towards publication.

This book will provide you with an in-depth view of what occurs behind the scenes in book publishing. It is important to know how a publisher will handle your book and how your hard work—sometimes a lifetime of work—can be damaged or destroyed through decisions often made by in-house staff without a thorough examination of the consequences. These decisions are sometimes made in an instant and are often intended to benefit a few interested parties, but end up being at the expense of many. Those affected have no recourse if they have only limited knowledge of industry basics and do not understand how publishers operate.

There is a big difference between being a writer and being an author. Writers love to write and write for the *sake* of writing. Authors are writers who have been *published*. Many writers become authors, yet remain writers because they are dedicated to their craft. They just happen to be published authors, but will forever remain writers. Some authors, somewhere along the line, decided publishing their work was all about obtaining notoriety and money. They forgot they were a writer first; their success in being published and, in a few cases, becoming a celebrity caused them to turn away from their craft. If you ever become an author, never forget what it was like to be a writer first—a struggling writer—and how you became an author.

There is yet another distinction between being a published author and a successfully published author. You will discover the difference as you read this book and you will be savvier about publishing, more informed about the process and armed with the knowledge that will help you to eventually become a successfully published author.

Please do not be disappointed I am not an editor or a publisher. Many writers do not realize the process of getting a book published is affected primarily by the last group to handle your book before publication: the marketing group that sells and distributes your work. To successfully navigate the publishing process, a writer must understand the influence of every person in every department who has a hand in publishing their book and especially how books are marketed and sold.

Part 1

WRITERS AND BOOKS

There are many ways of getting a manuscript published. Most writers hope to be published by a major publishing house, but that isn't the only avenue. Consider small publishers who offer more of a hands-on feel, or self-publishing where writers can control everything about their book. Most of all you must understand the market for selling and marketing books.

Publishing is a business and, as with any business, writers must know the ropes, understand the market and know how to deal with the people Involved. If you are an author who is not happy with the sales of your book or position with your publisher, then you need to know how to make the necessary changes.

"It's Only Books"

My sales group used to say, "It's only books." This was our way of reminding ourselves that publishing should be fun. We used to have a great time selling books. But somewhere along the line the industry lost sight of what was really important. The fun stopped, the course changed and generating revenue—not the authors or their books—became the priority.

Given the enormous amount of time and effort it takes for a writer to complete a book, publishers should handle as many as possible, with as much care as possible. However, that is not the reality of the corporate environment, especially when the owners of the largest publishers in the world happen to be among the biggest media conglomerates on the planet. The question every publisher, bookseller, author and writer should be asking is: What about the writers and the books?

Once you have finished your manuscript, what lies ahead can be as difficult and daunting as typing that first word was when you sat down in front of your computer. The next step is the culmination of your work, the big payoff, and the road is full of decisions. Do you self-publish? Should you start with a small press? Typically, writers are unaware of how such decisions can affect their book and, perhaps, their future.

The Major Houses

If you decide to find an agent and, hopefully, land a contract with a major publisher, remember that books are products. Knowing how your book should be packaged, priced or marketed and understanding how to make suggestions can help your book sales soar and give you a better chance at a lasting career as an author.

Once under contract to a publishing house, department heads will make the decisions concerning your book. If you want commercial success, fame and fortune, then you must understand that you always have a chance, but the opportunities are slim. Therefore, you cannot afford to rely on your publisher to make every decision about the publication of your book, though it is important that you follow certain guidelines. There is a right way and a wrong way to develop relationships with (and make suggestions to) your publisher.

Your Career as a Writer

If you want to make a living by writing, then success means success in the marketplace. Regardless of whether you decide to self-publish, go with a small house, or reach for the major publishers, this type of success can only come at the cash register. If you want a chance at getting your book published, at getting book buyers to purchase your second or third book in growing numbers and a chance at a career as a writer and author, then you need sales, not just publication and a spot on the bookstore shelf. Being able to say you are a published author does not mean that you are a successful author. *A successful author is proven by retail sales.*

A newly signed author is often fully confident that her new publisher will work magic to make her a best-selling author. However, she may not realize that by the time she has found an agent, editor and publisher—even before she has signed a contract—the mold for her book might already have been cast and will be handled according to established practices from that point on

Your manuscript being bought by a major house (or any house) is the end of one road and the beginning of another.

THE INDUSTRY

In recent years publishing has experienced slow growth for two reasons: fewer new retail booksellers are being developed and available retail space is being handed over to other products that sell faster and with higher profitability. Book publishing is a mature industry, one whose growth has been minimal when compared to our overall population growth.

Even though high profit margins for books make them attractive to booksellers, the major book retailers continue to stock shelves with an assortment of products like music, movies, magazines, greeting cards and writing journals, as well as adding coffee shops and bakeries. Books are not selling as well as they did twenty years ago and retail booksellers must increase their profits to say afloat.

Corporate expectations for book sales mirror expectations with electronics, food and an assortment of household consumer products. The customer base for books is relatively static; hence, growth means selling more books to the existing consumer at a time when cover prices are at their highest point. When you see industry figures being thrown about in the media, bear in mind that reference is being made to all types of publishing: textbook, specialty and general trade publishing. We all recognize the term "textbook" indicates sales to schools and universities, but "specialty publishing" refers to books published for markets such as associations, organizations, or non-profit corporations. Specialty also refers to books sometimes given away as promotional items to coincide with the launch of new products. This book deals only with general trade publishing in the traditional marketplace, where you will find books that appear prominently in national retail chains and on the major national bestseller lists.

Net unit sales in the publishing industry have been treading water every year over the past decade. Unit sales represent a single title and are representative of hardcover, trade paperbacks, mass market paperbacks and juvenile titles in all shapes and formats. That is not to say unit sales are dropping, but for the industry as a whole there has been a no-growth pattern in net unit sales in successive years. On the other hand, net dollar sales—the price of each unit sold at retail—managed to hold steady or, in some cases, even creep upward. If an individual company is fortunate and has a strong list of titles, they might see a slight increase in their overall gross dollar sales. This is a direct result of increases in the cover prices of individual books being sold at retail and not in the total number of individual copies sold.

Do not confuse gross dollar sales with net sales. Gross sales represent the total dollar amount of books shipped to booksellers for resale; net sales represent how many single copies were sold to the consumer or individual reader. The difference is the return factor (also referred to as sell-through or percent of sale), which, for an author, is critical to personal success.

The Price of Books

As the cover price of books continues to escalate, the corresponding number of units (or books) sold at retail will drop. This inverse relationship occurred over the course of many years and will continue to do so. Obviously, as cover prices increase, consumers buy fewer books. They visit their public library more often or trade books with friends, family and neighbors, rather than purchase their own copies of new releases. The proliferation in the number of used bookstores around the country is an indication of the consumer's adverse reaction to higher retail prices.

To explain the increases in cover prices, publishers cite the rising costs of producing, shipping and distributing a new book. What they do not mention is the escalating cost of doing business, where booksellers and book retailers demand more placement fees and advertising dollars to secure space in their stores. This cost is well beyond what would be considered reasonable when compared to the retail price of an individual book. Cost increases also result from highly inflated advances and royalties paid to a handful of authors. These payouts have increased dramatically for those who have been able to demand them. As big-name authors command more money per book, the limited resources of the publisher are being funneled to fewer writers and even fewer titles. This has a tremendously negative effect on the business overall and decreases opportunities for new authors and their profitability.

If these trends continue, there is a real threat that at some point rising cover prices and falling net unit sales may bring the industry to a crossroad where its survival will be at stake. Of course, there will always be books in some form. There are those who speculate that the technology of e-books (electronic books available only through the use of a computerized reader) will eventually erode consumers' desire to buy what we think of as a traditional bound book. At present, this theory has not held water. The technology is expensive. The cost of producing a limited number of e-books is high and the result is an excessive retail price acceptable only for those few buyers who want to own the latest thing.

There is something about the physical experience of a book—the printed words on a page, the cracking of the binding of a new book, the feel, weight and smell—that gives us hope the desire to read traditional books will be with us forever.

The Corporations

The largest trade publishing houses in the United States, which based in New York, are owned and controlled by multi-media entertainment conglomerates. Five of the top six are foreign-owned. This results in inherent conflicts. Advertising, in most cases, drives the multi-media companies that own book publishers. Advertising revenues from television, radio, magazines and the Internet are a big component in the revenue stream of those companies. Book publishers, on the other hand, are product-driven. They do not depend on advertising for revenue and there is no advertising placed in the books they publish. Therefore, the success or failure of a book depends on many factors beyond the rise and fall of advertising revenues.

If you wonder why publishers do not include advertising in their books, the politically correct answer might be that the practice would damage the integrity and credibility of the book. However, the real answer might be simply that books have never contained advertising. As the demands for growth increase, it is reasonable to assume that publishers will eventually find a way to attach some form of advertising revenue to the inside or even the front or back cover of some, or perhaps all, of their titles.

The Focus of Publishers

Generating revenue is the focus of all trade publishers. With a decline of independent bookstores in the past ten years and the shortage of retail space allotted to books at major mass merchants, publishers are trying to ship more copies to a shrinking market, resulting in a huge over-distribution situation. Shipping more copies than the market can absorb and causes book returns to increase. The rise in the total number of returns over the past decade is a clear indication publishers are shipping entirely too many copies to their customers.

Growth and success in the publishing industry depends on the editor's ability to attract and sign authors who have written the type of books the public wants to read. Luck plays a certain part in a publisher's success, but having a pulse on what readers want is important as well. Publishing often depends on the forces of the marketplace to create demand for certain titles. The motion-picture industry and television can have a tremendous influence on the shift of category and bestseller sales. Societal changes, major news events, cultural and religious attitudes and opinions also greatly influence what book publishers decide to print. The ability to foresee the ebb and flow of the world around us can have a dramatic effect on the sales success of the titles chosen for publication.

Big-Name Authors

Increasing sales through the acquisition of one of the "high-profile, best-selling" authors is difficult; they usually have strong ties to their current editors. They will, at times, follow their editors to a new publishing house, but switching houses forces the acquiring publisher to pay an enormous price. The price paid can result in millions of dollars being handed to the author for the right to publish their contracted books. This cost trickles down throughout the company and affects every aspect of the entire publishing process. It forces the publisher to funnel limited resources to a big name author, which takes away from the budgets that might have been dedicated to other titles and authors under contract. From a sales standpoint, it is difficult to make money when your company signs a big-name author.

When publishers persuade a major name to join their stable of authors, they often do so to enhance their company's credibility in the industry. This credibility can have a positive effect on the overall seasonal list of titles and may change the attitude that key book buyers have about a particular publishing house, or it can have no positive effect at all. In most cases, the huge cost of acquiring a best-selling author cuts deeply into a company's profits, hurting all the other authors and, in the end, may not be profitable.

Rather than attempt to win over current big-name authors, publishers press their editors to sign relative unknowns to a contract with hopes of turning a new book into a huge bestseller. Pushing large runs of a book by an author with a short and somewhat positive sales history is much more cost effective than trying to sign a bigger name author and making money on the publication of his or her next book.

I have seen this situation work both ways. I have watched books become huge bestsellers with a groundswell of pre-publication advertising and publicity and I've seen books that have fallen flat and remained on the shelves at retail. When the system works, everyone is a hero. When it doesn't, the incident is seldom ever mentioned again. Rarely do the mistakes of the past become lessons for avoiding them in the future. No one wants to talk about them. The thinking goes like this: if a book doesn't work, it doesn't mean it was a mistake, only that it didn't work at that particular time, in that particular season, on that particular list, with the combination of competing writers in existence at the time. Unfortunately, when this happens, the author quickly fades from memory.

Number of Titles Being Published

Corporate owners of the big publishing houses are constantly pushing for growth and profits, which results in larger numbers of individual books being shipped to the marketplace. It would seem logical that a company could grow their business by publishing more titles and shipping larger quantities of each book. However, over the past ten years the total number of titles being published by the major trade companies has actually dropped. Publishers tried to publish a larger number of individual titles in the late 80's and early 90's to the chagrin of their customers, the booksellers, who complained loudly because their shelves were too crowded already and, thus, managed to put a stop to the practice. Eventually, the number of titles on the seasonal lists declined, forcing publishers to concentrate on shipping more copies of existing titles. This was the start of today's current dilemma of over-shipping or over-distributing books into the retail marketplace.

Publishers desperate to grow their business and generate more revenue eventually fall into the trap of shipping more copies to the market than can be sold. There are many reasons for this, but the crux is that publishers must generate as much billing as possible. Being able to turn a book into a bestseller depends upon on the ability to sell a large number of copies to a wide distribution, which in turn gets the book noticed in numbers that justify its advertising and publicity costs. When this system fails, the company finds new ways of increasing orders, resulting in even more copies being shipped until eventually the industry operates in an overflow mode, glutted with books. What you end with is the current state of the business. Being published successfully means avoiding, or overcoming, this kind of situation.

THE PUBLISHER

Employees of the major trade publishers by and large are dedicated and qualified people. They make careers in publishing because they love books and the glamour associated with working in the industry. There is a certain mystique about working in a field with creative people and so the big companies end up with a highly educated, well-rounded, capable and motivated work force. Most staff and assistants in the various departments were born in the northeast, educated in the New England area and carry with them the bravado of those who were raised in and around the major metropolitan areas of the east coast. They are well read, often sophisticated and stay in tune with what is going on in the world of art, fashion and entertainment. Some are widely traveled and have many life experiences that add a demeanor to their work ethic, which can be construed as a touch of snobbishness.

Many people working in the publishing business are there because they knew someone who could make a phone call and get them an interview or they are related to someone inside the business. Initially they are hired because they need a job, not for the sheer love of books. Certainly, many employees got into the job by accident, but if they have been employed for any length of time, they have stayed because they fell in love with the business and all that surrounds the publishing of books. This is not to say they necessarily love authors. They merely love to read and enjoy a good book with a great story. As a result, they enjoy being around the business and the new books that arrive every single day.

Working with Authors

The majority of a publisher's employees never deal with authors, regardless of the authors' status. On occasion, the faithful get to attend a party held to honor a newly signed author or to toast the success of another big book by a recognized writer. Sometimes the staff's attendance signals that the invited media turned down an invitation and the house needed to boost the attendance to make it appear that the book was getting a lot of pre-publication attention. Regardless, this is the closest some employees will ever come to meeting or dealing with an author.

The authors who are most enjoyable to work with are the ones who are committed to their work and know how to show appreciation to everyone involved. They work hard at their craft and will only allow their book to be published when the story is satisfactory to all parties, not just for the sake of meeting a publishing schedule.

These are the authors who are genuinely interested in the job the staff does for them and will ask what they can do to help them do their job, which is to sell more books. These are the authors who remember what it was like to be a struggling writer.

Everyone who has worked in publishing for any length of time knows of or has met an author who was overly friendly and appeared excessively interested in who was responsible for moving their book along and what the staff had to say. These authors were most likely looking for a favor and had expectations the staff could not meet. They pretended to be friendly in the beginning, but when they failed to get the results they wanted they became critical of everyone and complained to their editor, who in turn complained to upper management that the staff was being uncooperative. As a new author, you never know who can help you or hurt you, so don't be one of these people. You will alienate the staff and everyone down the line.

For me, one of the most enjoyable parts of the publishing business was working with writers, listening to stories about how they got started, hearing the passion they had for their work and understanding their gift of creativity. Writers are the reason why most people who work in publishing want to continue to work there. They are what make the in-house staff work extra hard to make a book sell.

It doesn't matter if the employee will have any direct contact with the author; there is a certain amount of enthusiasm the entire house has when a book sells really well and generates lots of publicity. Everyone can sit back and say, "That's our book!" No group gets greater satisfaction out of seeing a book hit a national bestseller list than the staff people who actually do the work in-house. These folks take great pride in their job and want to do the best they can with every book and author. Unfortunately, the bigger picture can hinder this objective and certainly dampen the enthusiasm.

How They Treat You

How your book is treated in-house and ultimately how you, the author, are treated is often based on what the company paid for the rights to publish your book. If you received a large advance in the low six-figure range or above then you should have the full attention of everyone in the company. Your signing will most likely have appeared in the trade magazines, your local hometown newspaper and other publications or periodicals. If this is the case, then your book should command the attention it deserves. Now you need to make sure your book gets sold and distributed properly to booksellers.

If you were given an advance, let's say in the four-figures, then your book is among a group of titles the company needs to fill a publishing list. Your book is one of the hundreds of books a publisher buys and is vulnerable to mishandling due to the sheer size of a publishing list and the process through which your book must go to get published. If your book was bought for a low advance—something far short of what you'd need to devote yourself full-time to your writing—you might find it difficult to work through the maze of the publishing process. You will have to be realistic in your hopes of getting the distribution and attention you think your book deserves.

A Different Perspective

As you follow your book's progress from submission to publication, bear in mind those working in the staff and support positions in a New York trade publishing company live in and around the New York area. Those who were born and grew up there have a built-in set of perceptions about life, their environment and the rest of the world that anyone outside of New York might find hard to imagine. Believe it or not, this is one of the reasons editors and their staff can have a hard time relating to certain books about different ways of life in different parts of the country.

Someone raised in the west will have a certain set of perceptions about life that someone from New York could not possibly understand. So, if a good book comes along with a story about a person growing up in the Midwest, it is much harder for the New York types to grasp the language and culture than it would be for someone living west of the Hudson River. This is not to say that all books published have a built-in bias toward New York, but it does mean the publishing world, especially the New York publishing world, tends to see things differently than most everyone else.

This built in set of perceptions is something you need to try and understand, as a writer. Getting a feel for the people in-house and their nature will give you a better sense of how to make suggestions to your publisher. Making suggestions is important and making good recommendations can only be done if you understand your audience, the marketplace and something about the employees who work on your book.

Little Has Changed

The nuts and bolts of the business, the basics of how books are sold, marketed and distributed have changed little over the past twenty years. However, the way in which business is conducted has changed. You will find the most dramatic changes in the cost of doing business, the focus of the industry, the profit margins of the major retailers and, of course, the money spent on major authors. Publishers, by and large, are still trying to solve the same age-old problems they have had for decades with the same tired, worn-out solutions, struggling to grow a business nearly impossible to grow. The stable of consistent authors continues to face insurmountable odds, not only in the marketplace, but in-house as well. Corporate offices still apply pressure and still expect more and more, which forces an increased number of wrong decisions. Companies struggle to find ways to increase numbers and grow their business in an ever-shrinking environment.

Most everything about publishing seems to be stuck in the way things have been done for ages. There remains a certain standard: "It cannot be done because it has never been done." Those few people in the position to make changes seem reluctant to do so. There is an aversion to try new or different ways of conducting business. The industry has not evolved with the times. As a result, what was once a profitable and honorable business has turned into what has been described as a bad business model stuck in the past. Of course, I can't speak for all houses. My firsthand experience included two publishers and one national distributor. The fact remains that today nothing revolutionary is coming from any major publishing house. The only noticeable difference is that publishers are finding more creative ways to entice booksellers to buy more books than they can reasonably sell.

Who Holds the Power?

If there were ever an example of a business where the tail wags the dog, publishing would be it. Retailers and big-name authors hold the power and that power grows with each successive publishing season. The major houses pay entirely too much for a few best-selling books and bend over every which way to make the biggest authors happy. This comes at the expense of all the other authors under contract. It takes away resources in money and manpower that could be used to improve the chances of many other books to sell successfully.

Retailers and large booksellers have such power they can almost dictate terms. Moreover, the line between what is legal and what is not is so vague that, too often, in-house legal counsel must be consulted to make certain the marketing strategy for all book resellers is above-board. I'm not saying publishers are doing anything illegal, only that the line is blurred; there is not a lot of black or white, only a lot of gray. For example, meetings have been held where the purpose was to explain to the sales and marketing department what incentives they could and could not legally offer their customers.

Publishing at the major trade level and competition for spots on national bestseller lists such as the *New York Times*, is intense. Everyone is looking for an edge and the fight for publicity is incredible. Any author fortunate enough to land a five- or six-minute segment on a popular daytime talk show can multiply by thousands the number of copies their book will sell as a result. Compare that to a sixty-second commercial of the same title on the same show everyday for a week and the sales will not compare or even come close. Publicity sells books and the fight to get an author on the most popular shows is extremely competitive.

The marketplace can only absorb so many copies of a certain number of titles. The goal of all the big publishers is to ship as much as possible. When more copies of individual titles are shipped to secure shelf space, it creates an over-distribution situation where the retailers have few options but to return books quickly, which means a shorter shelf life for books that deserve a longer opportunity to sell.

The Hierarchy

As in any competitive business, the people who work at the grass roots level in publishing, the sales force, must be tough in order to survive. They fight the same battles over and over, year after year with many of the same customers. People in publishing, as in any large company, must be skilled in office politics. To get along and get things done they have to know who to schmooze, who to avoid, who they can trust and who they can't.

As a group, sales reps are spread around the country and most have not been raised or educated in the same circles as their colleagues from the New England area. They are the staff members who deal with customers day in and day out, the ones who have to fight company pressures and politics every day. They are the most street-wise of the in-house crew. As such, they are usually not caught up in the glamour of working in the publishing business, as are some New York-based personnel. These managers are the ones whose primary responsibility it is to find ways to increase billing, which means shipping more books to generate gross revenue. If there is one fact you should know, it's that the sales and marketing department can be your biggest ally or your worst enemy.

In today's publishing world the top executives have often risen to their positions from the sales or finance areas of the business. Few CEOs have strict editorial backgrounds and this has put a new face on the industry. Some say this is the root of the problems with over-distribution; the heads of the companies come from a background where shipping large numbers of copies keeps them in their comfort zone and in the biggest chair at the table. This allows them to retain their top job through shipping many copies in an attempt to generate growth rather than acquiring, nurturing and supporting new talent in the form of new writers.

Typically, most publishing executives started somewhere lower in the company and worked their way up the ladder through years of hard work and sacrifice. These companies, as well as the industry as a whole, are incestuous. Rarely, if ever, do top executives of major trade publishing houses come from any other industries. Top executives switch from one publishing company to the next, as do many department heads. Rarely do the top spots go to people outside the business of publishing. Most have degrees in the Arts and Sciences, English or literature, not business. A surprising number of executives may not even have a college degree.

This is the business of publishing; experience speaks louder than formal education or top positions in other industries. Some say that publishing is so specialized the CEO of a consumer product company could not be successful in the same position at a trade publisher. Perhaps that is true, but publishing needs to attract more outside business people to help solve many of the industry's woes.

AGENTS AND EDITORS

If your goal as a writer is to land a contract with one of the large publishing houses then the most recognizable way of doing this is to obtain the literary services of an agent. It is possible to attract the attention of a large trade publisher without an agent. There have been many self-published authors who have been successful at selling books and were eventually pursued by a major publisher. Two most notable examples with my former company were James Redfield and *Celestine Prophecy* and Robert Kiyosaki with *Rich Dad, Poor Dad*. However the vast majority of writers utilize an agent to introduce their work to publishers.

Finding the right agent, writing the proper query letter and submitting your manuscript in a way that will guarantee results is well beyond the scope of this book. My experience with agents was limited, in most situations, to explaining why an author failed to find his or her book in certain retail locations.

There is no doubt that agents are a key component in getting your manuscript published, but there should also be no doubt with whom the agents are most closely aligned. There are tens of thousands of writers who want to be authors, but there are only a handful of major trade publishers that have the capability to make your book a national bestseller. Agents need the close contacts with key editors in positions where they can get the most money for their clients: you, the writer. The well-known agents represent many writers and authors and they do what is best for their reputation in the eyes of the publisher, not necessarily the writer.

Good Agents and Bad Agents

There are many wonderful agents who do everything they can for their clients and work extremely hard to land them the best possible publishing contract available. They stay on top of the business; they know what is selling and where; they maintain a close relationship with the major editors and key players in every major house in New York. They have the ability to pick up the phone and make an immediate appointment with just about anyone. But be aware of who works closely with whom. The agents need to maintain good relationships with editors much more than they do with any individual writer. Any agent who attempts to play hardball too often with key publishers or editors might find they are unable to get their clients' work published. Such is the nature of the business.

Finding the right agent, one who understands your work and is willing to work with you to build a career, is the first step in getting your book published by a major house. The process of finding and signing with an agent can itself be difficult. Agents are known to specialize in certain categories of books. Choosing the right agent for yourself and your book is critical. You want to make certain the agent you select has a history with authors who are published in the same genre as yourself. The wrong agent can send you down a road to disaster and could jeopardize your career as a writer and successful author. Seek advice from people who have worked behind the scenes or from other published authors.

You Need an Objective Evaluation

An agent should be someone who can honestly evaluate your writing and identify your place in the genre and mix of successfully published authors. An agent's goal should be to find the right publisher for your work, not just the one willing to pay the largest advance. Don't be fooled by someone who tells you that just getting published is the key. The truth is that you need to be published successfully and success means selling copies, not simply having the book show up on store shelves. Being published by the wrong publisher with a bad reputation for how they handle authors or how they sell and distribute books can be the absolute worst way to gain entry into the industry.

You need to find an agent and a publisher with a proven track record of turning manuscripts like yours into bestsellers. An agent's introduction of your manuscript to an editor and their discussions about your book are important steps towards becoming a published author. Often those discussions set the foundation for how that house decides to publish your book. You need an agent who can get your manuscript in front of the right editors who will want to buy your book, an agent who will negotiate a contract that will give you the best opportunity to be successful. After a successful negotiation and signed contract, you will become a published author. For some writers, success is simply getting published. If this is your goal, then at the point you sign a contract you will be a success. If your goal is to sell books, then find the right agent, or go it alone and self-publish. Learn how to generate publicity and sell books. Selling your book is the bottom line, so discover how to market and promote your work and you can be successful regardless of who publishes your work.

Unsolicited Manuscripts

Patience in finding the right agent is as important as signing a contract with the right publisher.

Agents love the fact that the major trade publishers do not accept unsolicited manuscripts for consideration. An agent must deliver every manuscript that ends up on the desk of an editor. This is why publishers need agents: to bring them manuscripts they can publish. Editors spend a lot of time courting the hottest agents because they want first crack at the best manuscripts. The hottest are the ones who are fortunate enough to have a stable of best-selling authors, or who represented the most recent member to the national bestseller club, an author whose book is currently the talk of the cocktail party crowd. It's a "we need each other" relationship: agents need editors in key positions at major publishers and editors need hot agents to bring them the latest and best manuscripts.

Publishers always need new manuscripts they can turn into books. They must have a constant in-flow of product. The reason for not accepting unsolicited manuscripts is because of copyright laws and fear of lawsuits. As a result, an agent must submit your manuscript to the house. There is a professional responsibility on the part of agents to bring publishers the original work of an author. The so-called "slush pile," the stack of unsolicited manuscripts that show up in publishers' mailboxes every day does not really exist at the major trade level. Any unsolicited manuscripts that arrive in the mail at a major New York trade publisher will be returned to the sender unopened.

Next, the Editor

Most editors with whom I have worked closely over the years are wonderful people, intelligent, obviously well read, good conversationalists with a keen sense of humor, devoted to their work. But, like some writers, there are editors looking for the next company promotion or article in the trade magazines with their name prominently displayed rather than trying to attract and develop new writers. It is not difficult to distinguish the two.

The job of an editor is to recognize talent and use her expertise to turn a manuscript into a book that will make the company money. A good editor is someone who has their finger on the pulse of what is new and exciting in our world, who can spot a writer with an ability to tell stories or transfer thoughts. They can identify trends and have the ability to work well with all departments in-house and the skills to help the writer mold their work in such a way that gives it the best chance to sell as many copies as possible. Discovering new talent—new writers who offer a distinctive voice—is a very important part of an editor's job. Editors are always on the lookout for new writers because the company is in constant need of new product. When it comes to editing your book, it is the editor who determines whether what you've written is believable, reads well, has its own rhythm and whether your characters are sympathetic. A great editor not only serves the publisher, but also helps you shape your book in such a way that the reader will embrace what you have written. This translates into book sales. In-flow of new product and new product sales is what pays the bills, generates revenue and keeps the corporate watchdogs happy. So, when your editor suggests rewrites or raises questions about your characters, storyline, or intention, take their questions and advice seriously.

Honesty Helps Sell Books

Members of the sales and marketing team appreciate editors who are honest in their presentation and facts. Too often editors stretch the truth at marketing meetings in hopes their books will be bought and get better positioning on the seasonal list of titles. However, the truth about a book will always come out because as the sales group prepares to present new titles they always do extensive research on the sales history of the author, if one exists. Editors who constantly clamor that their titles are the next bestseller when none of their books can be separated from the others end up getting little attention in-house.

When you first sign that publishing contract, your editor is the only link you have to the rest of the company. As you move forward through the publishing process, it will be important for you to become aware of your editor's in-house reputation as well as which people in the other departments have a hand in the publication of your book.

When an editor decides your manuscript is worthy of purchase she will make a presentation to the editorial or publishing committee. That committee will decide whether or not to buy your book. When the editor makes the decision to present your manuscript for consideration she is in essence putting her reputation on the line. Your editor's decision-making ability and eye for a good book is at stake every time they make a recommendation to buy a manuscript. They cannot afford to offer too many books that eventually fail to make money. This will reflect badly on their career.

The Editor's Reputation

The recent number of bestsellers an editor has edited often determines his or her reputation industry-wide and especially in-house. This is, of course, a direct reflection of their ability to spot talent and turn books into bestsellers.

For example, if your editor has not had a best-selling book in recent memory, the employees who have a hand in bringing your book to market will typically not go the extra mile to make certain it sells a lot of copies. That means your manuscript will not be given the importance it probably deserves, simply because the editor is not held in high regard by his or her colleagues.

An editor with a reputation for offering larger than expected advances could be a prime target for an agent. Obviously, this is a bonus for you as an author, but is often frowned upon by everyone in-house. You have to sell enough books to repay the advance out of your royalties. If the advance is excessive, it may be years before the amount is paid and you begin collecting royalties on a regular basis. You are at the mercy of everyone in-house and your situation is dependant on the reputation of your editor.

The in-house credibility of an editor garnered from his or her success at picking books is what is most important to you as a new author. This is impossible for you to know unless you do your research after your agent discloses which editor is getting a copy of your manuscript. Do some homework to develop a list of the authors this editor works with and then check the shelves of the local bookstore to see if copies of books by these authors are readily available. If not, your editor may be on a collision path with a career change, which could leave you suddenly without an editor, even if temporarily.

This is why it is important for you to know your genre, which authors sell the best, which publishers have the most books and which editors handle the best-selling authors. You cannot possibly know the reputation of an editor prior to your introduction by an agent; however, you can get a sense of what's to come by familiarizing yourself with your genre.

BOOK BUYERS

Book buyers are the individuals who work for the large retailers whose job it is to purchase books for their company. The single biggest component of a publisher's marketing efforts is through the book buyer. In today's competitive climate, marketing directly to the buyer whose company has the largest number of retail outlets is common.

The decisions and influence that a few book buyers have on what America reads may be surprising. Fortunately, their knowledge and experience about what they are doing makes most of their decisions credible. When questions arise about the larger than normal quantity of purchase for an individual title, you can almost always point to the corporate office of the publisher and bookseller, where a deal might have been cut to warehouse books. As odd as it seems, the famous authors selling the most books benefit from large buys and the new authors suffer, no matter how good their book.

Consider for a moment the fact that only a handful of book buyers across the industry are responsible for what America is offered in major retail booksellers across the country. A publisher's sale of any title is concentrated in the hands of a few book buyers. These represent the bulk of the order on any individual title.

Unfortunately this is business, the part of publishing that hurts deserving new authors more than anything.

Coveting the Buyers

Unfortunately, the publishers' overwhelming desire to generate revenue has eroded the decision-making ability of the most knowledgeable buyers and too often ends up in the hands of the accountants and financial folks. The chances of a new author getting the attention of these key book buyers is based entirely on the marketing efforts of their publisher, but for the most part this attention happens only on rare occasions.

Most of these buyers have a solid book background with years of experience in the industry and, for the most part, are voracious readers themselves. Of course, they have their own personal likes and dislikes when it comes to the books they read. Sometimes the buyer is fortunate enough to buy books in a category he or she personally likes. Buyers have been accused, on occasion, of allowing their personal bias to affect their purchase decisions. In certain situations, that bias may be reflected in the category and quantity of books they buy.

Book buyers may also have salespeople they like and dislike. They may favor or object to a sales representative based on the person's personality and professionalism (or lack thereof) or even based on whether the buyer likes or dislikes the sales management of the company. These personal feelings can and do, affect buyers' purchases, especially when there are two competitive titles that have similar sales histories or potential to sell at retail. Depending on the size of the company for whom the book buyer works, the bias they have could jeopardize a sales rep's bonus, performance review, or even their hope of moving up the ladder.

Finding Common Ground

Sales reps must be careful to get along with their book buyers, because they must deal with these people on a regular basis, selling to them again and again, possibly over many years. Publishing is very much a relationship business and one that typically has taken years to develop and nurture. If a publisher finds that a sales rep is not getting along with a particular buyer, then the company may reassign that rep to another customer.

The relationship between a book buyer and a publisher can be influenced by many factors. One factor is management or personality style; sometimes a publisher just can't get along with a bookseller's management and, thus, the relationship can be strained, as may happen in any business situation.

Relationships can become strained in a number of ways. One of the more common in the publishing business is when a publisher "goes over the buyer's head" to upper management in an attempt to gain an advantage on the buy of a particularly difficult book. The publisher will offer incentives for the bookseller to make a larger than normal purchase. This happens more often than sales representatives would like and the results are usually disastrous. A publisher may get the buy it wants on one book to meet an in-house budget and revenue goal, but buys on other books throughout the seasonal list will always suffer as a result.

Buyers Love Books

Most book buyers love books, love to read and enjoy the business. Book buyers do their job because they love it, not because they hope to get rich. Good buyers will have an intuitive sense about a book, either from the packaging or the manuscript. They are typically overwhelmed with the number of manuscripts they receive. Their offices are usually filled with stacks and stacks of reading copies. Getting a book read by an influential book buyer is difficult because their choices are usually too numerous for any one book to get singled out and this is why it is important for publishers to market directly to the key book buyers. This has become the most cost effective way to gain attention for the more important titles.

Writers should have an understanding of how buyers purchase books and the dynamics that play a part in a buyer's decision. If a publisher needs to receive an exceptionally large order from an important book buyer at a key bookseller, the publisher's representative will do everything to win that person over. Marketing directly to the buyer of a major bookseller is a key part of the overall marketing plan for titles. These people are often courted with all sorts of spiffs. Whether the buyer purchases the book at levels the company wants or needs without a special offer usually boils down to whether the book has the potential to sell copies in abundance, as well as the publisher's support. However, in today's market climate the buy on that book may also be reflected on the allowance or fee a publisher is willing to pay the bookseller to make an unusually large purchase on a specific title.

A book purchased at a low number does not necessarily mean the book is not expected to sell at retail. There are many factors that influence the buy on a book from a major bookseller. Timing is critical; the buy can be affected by the release date of a competing author for any given publication month. The key to being published successfully will depend on where the book is being distributed as well as the initial purchase from the assortment of booksellers.

It's a Relationship Business

As with most businesses, publishing is a relationship business. Sales reps can survive and succeed if they have a strong relationship with booksellers and their book buyers. It is important to gain insight into the world of the salesperson whose job is to sell books and to work closely with a buyer.

These relationships can be fragile and should be based on respect and honesty. A sales rep will sell to the same buyer each month or each season and often speaks to them several times a week via phone or e-mail. Being dishonest about a publisher's true intent regarding a title, or trying to mislead the buyer with faulty sales history, is a surefire way for a rep to create an environment of distrust. Buyers deal with many salespeople and they have to depend on the reps to be truthful about their books and sales history. Buyers do not have time to research each and every book sold to them.

Once that line is crossed, between truth and the not so true and the buyer does not feel he or she can trust what the salesperson has to say, the result is a slippery slope from which it is almost impossible to recover.

Buyers Can Change Employers

It is not unusual for a book buyer to switch companies. A good buyer can, over the course of a few years, end up working with more than one bookseller. A salesperson can help maintain his respectability by being knowledgeable about his titles. But the willingness to be truthful with the buyer is the biggest difference between a good rep and just an average rep.

Often, the salesperson will have to sell a certain book by a particular author. Both parties know the author's previous title sold a certain number of net copies, yet the company's budgeted title for the new book is substantially higher than the previous book. How can the rep expect to ask for a large increase in the next buy without looking like a complete idiot? The first thing he'll have to do is be honest with the buyer and tell the truth—that his company feels this next book has the potential to sell a certain net number and he needs an increased buy. The sales rep must then provide as much supporting information as possible to make it easier for the book buyer to make a positive decision.

Explaining the potential is the difficult part and it needs to be more than "a feeling the company has for the book." This is where the additional advertising, promotion, or publicity over and above the last book comes into play. If the rep asks for the bigger number and has nothing to back up his request, the rep's credibility can often be the only remaining chip with which to bargain.

Favors

There are times when buyers will call a sales rep asking for a certain favor; it can be something personal, such as wanting a book for a friend, family member or a child. It might even be something professional such as shipping an important title early to gain an advantage on competitive booksellers. Either way, the sales rep is usually more than glad to try and accommodate the buyer, depending on the size of the account. This is another bargaining chip used when getting a bigger buy on another book.

Hopefully, the rep will have sent an advance reading copy to his buyer long before he'd have to sit down and ask for a higher number on any title. He'd also hope his buyer will have read the copy and liked it. The buyer will ask how the house justifies the higher number and how the publisher plans to support the book.

During the course of the budget process, the rep hopes that, in-house, his company is committed to additional advertising and promotion. This way he can give the buyer a straightforward and honest answer that clearly indicates the company is behind the author and can support the new number.

Sometimes he gets the support he needs and sometimes he doesn't. If the rep walks in and tells them he has this book that his company paid a lot of money for and needs their support, he will have less chance of getting what he needs. Buyers don't necessarily like a book for which the author received a large advance or one for which the author has no track record of net sales to support the big bucks.

They also do not like being asked to support a book with a larger purchase than was made for the author's last title without some sort of additional support from the company. The question will be, if the publisher feels so strongly about this book why aren't they behind it with more advertising or a bigger author tour?

This is just a brief glimpse of some of the situations salespeople face on a daily basis. Keep this in mind when you ask for explanations on numbers, distribution and everything else that affects your book's success. The key to obtaining the right distribution, which gives a book the best opportunity to sell, can ultimately rest on the relationship the salesperson has with a book buyer.

BOOKSELLERS

In order to gain a clear understanding of book distribution and its importance in selling your book, you need to know something about the various booksellers, their function and how they operate in the marketplace. Depending on the genre, format and price of your book, some booksellers offer the author a better chance at selling copies than others.

Retail Chain Bookstores

Publishers sell books to a variety of customer types. The most commonly recognized are the large national retail bookstore chains (such as *Barnes & Noble* or *Borders*), which account for the greatest combined percentage of a publisher's business. They dominate the attention and the resources of the publisher. They also buy the widest assortment of titles, which adds depth to the list and gives more authors an opportunity to have their titles displayed and sold. A major trade publisher must have a certain amount of exposure for its titles in these retail bookstores.

When you walk into any of the recognizable national retail booksellers, keep in mind that virtually every square inch of the store is for rent. The floor and table displays of best-selling books are rented for a specific period of time. Titles facing up on a table get stacked that way because the publisher paid for the placement.

National bookstore chains are a great place to have

your book distributed. This is a destination market for readers buying books. However, if you are self-published or with a small press and are fortunate to have your book bought by these chains, you will more than likely have a better chance of being successful and selling copies if you focus the distribution to your own local region of the country where you live, or in the vicinity of where your book is based (if that is an important part of your book). You have the best chance of selling more net copies in big retail bookstores than the other booksellers. Getting distribution to these stores in the right locations is important.

Membership Clubs

Another large segment of a publishers business are large discount club stores where a membership is required (like *Costco* or *Sam's Club*). These competitors offer consumers large quantities of best-selling books, often at prices well below what most other retailers can offer. In fact, in some instances, these retailers sell books at or below their own cost.

The large discount club stores typically want only the best-selling titles in large quantities. Their remaining titles are usually books with vague regional appeal, or older backlist titles that tie into an author's new book. Others have been in print for some time and continue to sell at predictable levels. With these booksellers, the biggest problem facing publishers is that a title must sell large quantities fast or the copies are returned quickly. These booksellers are only concerned with books that sell in numbers large enough to maintain the small space the store provides; otherwise, they will take the title out of inventory and return it to the publisher to make room for the next title.

These accounts have strict limits on the number of SKU's for books (barcodes assigned to the back cover of each individual book). They can inventory only so many titles in so much quantity and they must turn the inventory quickly. If you were a new author and had a chance to distribute large quantities of your book into these accounts, be careful. It would be wise again to limit your distribution to a region of the country where you live or work or where your book is based. One wrong move in these stores and your total net sale could be a disaster.

Mass Merchants

Next are the large discount retail chains, or mass merchants, the ones you see in any major city around the country (*Wal-Mart* or *Target,* for example). These dominant big-box retailers want the major bestsellers as well as a few selected mid-list category books and a few backlist titles to tie in with a new book from a known author. On occasion they will offer a title with regional appeal but seldom will give any attention to new authors unless the enticement from the publisher is strong enough.

Even though these retail discount chains are known for the low prices and wide assortment of merchandise, they are not aggressive with their marketing of books. They devote space only because they like the residual value and profit a book can contribute to their bottom line. They are not a major player. They do sell bestsellers well, but so does every other bookseller in the country. They do not promote an individual title through special displays and in-store advertising; the cost of participating in this kind of promotion can be prohibitive.

Once again, if, as a new author, you have an opportunity to have your book distributed to these stores, be careful. They also need to turn inventory quickly. They depend on large amounts of in-store advertising and promotion for books to be successful. Unless your book is on the store's bestseller list or getting special promotional attention, try to avoid as much distribution to these stores as possible.

Book Jobbers

After the large national retail bookstore chains, the discount clubs and big box discount retailers, come the book jobbers (such as *Ingram* or *Baker and Taylor*). For the publisher, the jobber is a place to warehouse books at the time of publication. They need copies in these accounts to re-supply the smaller customers when a book takes off. They supply retail customers, small independent bookstores—and, in some cases, the chain stores—with new titles, as well as any reorders. They supply the library market with new titles. Jobbers also buy books for small bookstores that do not have the time or manpower to order for themselves and depend on the jobber to make their book buying decisions.

Jobbers are important to publishers because they make it easier for a small bookstore to reorder a best-selling title without having to deal directly with the individual publisher. A small store can make one phone call and get all the reorders they need. The best way for publishers to reach the multitude of smaller customers is through a book jobber.

If a large percentage of your distribution is being shipped to jobbers, then you have a big problem. Large numbers of books sold to jobbers without corresponding large orders from retailers are out of balance and can create large return problems for authors. Booksellers need a demand at the retail level to pull books through their system so they can turn their inventory fast enough to prevent excessive returns. Large quantities of books in jobbers are only as good as the corresponding numbers in bookstores and other retail booksellers.

Independent Distributors

Another class of customer is wholesalers, referred to in the industry as independent distributors (IDs) whose primary responsibility is providing magazines to local supermarkets, drug stores, airport terminals, military bases and convenience stores (an example is *Charles Levy*). Books represent a small piece of this group's total business, with magazines being their dominant source of revenue. An ID that pays attention to books will place a rack of books somewhere in the aisles of their customer, typically a supermarket. In some cases the percentage of their business represented by book sales can climb to as much as 20%, but generally this is not the case. Books usually represent somewhere around 10% to 12% of their total business.

There are only three major companies, all grounded in the book and magazine distribution business that represent the major ownership of the ID's in the United States. These customers rarely go more than a few titles into any publisher's mass market paperback list and will pick only the cream of the crop in trade paper and hard covers. Their bread and butter for books is tied to promotions, whether it is the book on which a major motion picture is based, or the latest and hottest author.

IDs typically have the highest rate of returns for books of any bookseller. Try to avoid these accounts unless your book is part of a larger promotion. These retailers are not in tune with books, do not promote books properly and usually do a poor job of selling any titles beyond the major bestsellers. If you are the author of a category title and are getting minimal overall distribution then you do not want your title in these stores. Avoid it at all costs!

Independent Bookstores

Next are the independently owned local bookstores that have managed to survive despite the onslaught of competition and continue to be the backbone of the traditional publishing industry. Independent bookstores, those locally owned and operated, have decreased in number dramatically over the past few years

To understand the importance of independent bookstores, consider first the large retail chain bookstores. These stores are mirror images of themselves. Go to any store, browse the aisles and then drive a few miles to the next one and you will see virtually the same thing: The same mix of titles, with few exceptions. However, go to an independent bookstore and you will find a whole new world opened to the reader. This is truly what bookselling is all about.

Independent bookstores are the last real hope for new authors who are trying to break into the world of publishing. These stores are certainly more willing than the chains to give newer authors a chance to prove themselves. They also want to make titles available to their customers that are not readily offered by their national competitors. Unfortunately for aspiring writers, the loss in the total number of independent bookstores throughout the country diminishes the opportunities they have to get their book published and offered to the reading public.

If your book is being distributed to only one retail

bookseller, the independent bookstore is the place to be. They typically have the highest sell-through percentage of all booksellers, they pay more attention to detail, their staff is more knowledgeable and they promote books better than any of the other major booksellers, including the major chain bookstores. If your actual first print is a few thousand copies, do everything you can to convince your publisher that you first want distribution to independent bookstores around the country before any other bookseller.

Internet Booksellers

Internet companies are not to be overlooked. As we all know, there is one large online seller, one medium sized seller owned by one of the major bookstore chains and several smaller ones (*Amazon* and *Barnesandnoble.com*). Don't be fooled by what you might read or hear about selling books on the Web. Publishers pay to be listed on these Web sites, and pay dearly. As with the shelf space inside a retail bookstore, it's all about real estate and there is definitely a cost of renting that space, whether it is on the Web or inside a brick-and-mortar store.

Internet sellers typically do not order large quantities of books. They order enough to fill their immediate demand and then turn to jobbers for the re-supply. As a total percent of a publisher's first print, these online stores are small. However, the presence of books on these sites is important for the exposure necessary to gain attention from the market and drive consumers into other retail booksellers.

If your publisher is willing to pay for the promotion necessary to get your book placed with Internet booksellers, then go for it. This is a terrific place to get exposure.

However, you do not want large quantities of your total in print to be distributed to Internet booksellers. All you want is the exposure. However, it is costly and may not fit into the budget of your publisher.

Specialty Retailers

Finally, there is an assortment of retail stores that fills the needs of smaller specialty markets such as gardening and cooking stores that require an occasional book in their stores. These represent a small percentage of the overall traditional trade book business. Publishers sometimes sell to them through a separate group within the company often known as the special sales department. These small specialty markets add up to a huge number in overall book sales.

The many booksellers listed above are the customers that dominate the sales and attention of the major trade publishers. If you were wondering about all the other avenues of book sales, know that outside of the group mentioned above, the major publishers do not have the time, resources or manpower to even attempt to sell books to any other market. This is the business of trade publishing.

It's important to keep in mind that each book customer can play a significant role in the sale of your book. Understanding their importance and how distribution to these various booksellers fits into your goal is important in maximizing the net sale of your book.

Part 2

THE ACQUISITION

After your agent has submitted your manuscript to an editor and the editor has decided to present it to the editorial committee, a meeting is held to discuss its potential. New acquisitions meetings take place on a regular basis in which all potential acquisitions are discussed in terms of profit and loss and how that book might do in the marketplace. At that meeting a profit and loss (P&L) statement is passed around so everyone can see what kind of money the company hopes to make on that book. The editor, with the aid of the finance department, will have put together the preliminary P&L statement based on facts gathered from a variety of sources. Too many times those sources do not include the sales department.

Editors' Preparation

In preparation for the meeting, editors will do everything they possibly can to make sure the best light is placed on the author and the manuscript. Regardless of whether the author has a sales history for previously published books, the editor will compare the writing to as many best-selling writers and the corresponding sales history as they possibly can. The fact that any editor would even attempt to conceal the actual sales of an author is beyond me, because the real numbers are always discovered in the end.

If you are a proven author, meaning you have written other books and have developed a sales history, then sales numbers used in the P&L should have a better chance of being valid, but often that is not the case. Occasionally editors use sales numbers from a prospective author's agent, rather than from actual cash register sales provided by major retailers. It has been my experience that often the numbers provided by an agent have been inaccurate. Of course, you would have to wonder about the accuracy of such numbers, since the agent has a vested interest in making the author's sales look good.

The financial information presented at the editorial (acquisitions) meeting gives everyone an idea of how many copies the company expects to distribute, how many they hope to sell, how many will be reordered and what they hope the sell-through percentage will be. All of this is based on the editor's best guess and, again, too often without any initial input from sales.

The editor will argue that the advance needed to purchase the rights to the book is reasonable based on past sales of the author's books (if these exist), how well similar books have sold, or simply the editor's instincts. The editor will also argue that the favorable comparison to other current best-selling or successfully published authors is warranted.

The Decision

At each of these editorial meetings a number of titles will be discussed. Decisions are made based on a variety of factors. Certainly, there are financial considerations, but decisions can also depend on the category or genre of a book, the time of year the editor wants to publish, how many books in the same category the company has bought and scheduled for publication at the same time, and on and on.

Again, your editor's in-house credibility plays a role in the decision. So, if you've had a book turned down by a publisher, keep in mind that timing is always important and may have accounted for the decision, rather than the quality of your book.

The bottom line factors on most decisions to buy a manuscript are: (1) can the company sell this book in sufficient quantities to make money, (2) can the company promote the author (is the person presentable? can the company send this person out on the road to sell their book?), and (3) does the company have any other similar titles under contract? Whether or not a company decides to buy your manuscript, the decision is often based on these three important points. Finally, an offer is made and accepted, the agent is happy, you are elated and the publisher starts to work.

SCHEDULE FOR PUBLICATION

After your manuscript has been purchased and you signed a contract, your book is added to the agenda of the next meeting where the publishers, editors and sales department will sit down to schedule your title for publication. Typically, books are published anywhere from eighteen months to three years after their purchase. This gives the company plenty of time to make preparations and it gives the writer adequate time to complete the book or make revisions, whatever is appropriate, according to the wishes of the editor.

Books are not scheduled haphazardly; a lot of thought and discussion goes on behind the scenes. Great pains are taken to make sure the publication date is good for the company, which should, in turn, make it good for the author and their book. Publishers go to great lengths to make sure their seasonal lists of titles are balanced. The goal is to offer the book buyer a wide range of category selection on the seasonal list. Every list needs to be well-rounded, which means an adequate representation of novels, non-fiction, category titles, biographies, cookbooks…you get the idea. They also want to make sure they do not have too many new authors or ones that lack sufficient positive sales history.

Dormant Period

Once your manuscript has been bought and scheduled for publication, the preparation for all the other titles under contract continues. During this eighteen to thirty-six month dormant period, your book sits. Eventually, your cover will be created, production work started and preparation will be made for your book to be positioned, sold and shipped.

This dormant period is the most critical time for you, the author, because you must take advantage of this time to develop relationships with everyone who has a hand in the production of your book. Don't waste this period basking in the fact that you are going to be a published author, you need to start separating yourself and your book from the rest of the other titles on the seasonal list by developing relationships, gradually moving to the decision makers and becoming known as an author who is willing to do anything and everything necessary to help sell your book.

There is a timeline for your book's publication and unless something dramatic happens, your book is slotted and moving towards an on-sale date. You must consult with your editor to confirm the completion dates. Prior to this point, you need to reach out to those with whom you have developed relationships and offer suggestions. Once the dormant period ends, it's too late to make changes to your book, so if you want to have a successful sale, take advantage of this time.

Several Imprints

Each publisher typically has several imprints, more specialized divisions inside the larger company, each using a different name and logo under which it publishes titles. A given publisher might have several major imprints, which means it publishes, for example, a full list of fiction, non-fiction and so forth. There are also category imprints focusing on mystery, science fiction, romance and of course, children's books. My former company also had an imprint for what we called the coffee table books, those large, odd-sized art and photo books with high price points.

Occasionally, different imprints within the same house may compete for the right to publish the same book. When this happens the publishers of either imprint typically work well together for the greater good of the company. Usually the one who ends up purchasing the book has a particular editor with a reputation for publishing that type of book more effectively than an editor at the sister imprint.

In total, the number of titles any one publisher produces in a year can be from over a hundred to several thousand, so when a seasonal list of titles is being developed, it is important the publisher makes sure to have a strong lineup of books that are well-rounded and cover a wide range of categories.

Anchor Titles

Every list needs anchors, those big titles that will provide the company with the largest initial orders and thus represent the biggest chunk of billing. These titles are certain to receive widespread support, generate big orders and (everyone hopes) bring in a lot of revenue to the company. A seasonal list without a sufficient number of anchors is a list destined for obscurity. Major publishers will typically have at least one major author every single month and should have, to remain competitive, two or three major books every month.

A lot of coordination takes place to make sure the list for each imprint is balanced by month so the company is not competing against itself. For example, if two similar imprints within a house were both trying to publish each one's biggest author during the same month, they could drain purchases and revenue away from each other, so the company would not schedule two big books by mega-authors in the same month.

If the expectations for the book are high enough, key book buyers may be consulted for advice on where a particular book or author should be scheduled. If the publisher can get a recommendation from a buyer as to the best schedule, the publisher can later use that fact with the buyer when it comes time to place an order.

Competition is a huge factor in publication schedules. No one has a crystal ball that reveals the competition's seasonal publishing schedule. Certainly, when competitors announce release or on-sale dates for their biggest books, a publisher may decide to juggle their own schedule to try and give a certain title a better competitive advantage. Books are moved around in a schedule to give them the best possible opportunity at the time of publication to maximize the sale at the booksellers' cash register. These decisions are based on all the relevant factors the company has to work with at the time.

Timing of the Publication

You may have noticed that certain authors are published at certain times of the year. This is how the company spreads the wealth and anchors its lists. Publishers may schedule "big" books for important seasons. For example, the fall (beginning after Labor Day) is always an ideal time for publishers because of the holiday season and the foot traffic in stores. Some of the really big authors are being published three times a year, one book each publishing season. That may be great for the company and the bottom line, but it is not so good for the chances of a new author trying to break rank and get a good position on the publisher's seasonal list.

Risk and risk aversion are behind the thinking of some individuals who develop the publishing schedule. When books are juggled and publishing schedules set for a new season, decisions are not necessarily about the books and certainly not about an author's future. The list of titles has to fit together to form the company's best opportunity to generate as much billing in the form of large initial orders as possible. The seasonal list is scheduled for its ability to generate revenue, not what is best for any individual title or author. Every book plays a part of the total package. The seasonal list of titles and securing the most revenue from each book is what is most important in the minds of the publishers.

On occasion, a faster route to market takes place when the rights to a book are purchased and it's immediately added to an existing seasonal list currently being sold to book buyers. This means that book is being "crashed" and everything has to be done quickly so the book can be sold right away. This can happen to any author regardless of the time of year, category, or advance and may or may not be a good thing for the book and the author.

The decision whether to crash a book can depend on many factors. Most often a book is crashed because another author did not meet a deadline and the company needs a replacement. Sometimes it is simply for financial reasons. If an agent tells you that your book is perfect for a publisher to crash their current seasonal list, you would be wise to discover the factors surrounding the move. Before your agent agrees to a contract, find out how it would benefit your book. The reasons behind a book being crashed and sold immediately are important to know. Depending on the book and the particular circumstances, crashing could be a good thing for the book and for you, or it could be a bad thing.

Size of the Market

The marketplace for books is only so big, which means there are only a limited numbers of slots for books in the traditional retail marketplace. There are only so many titles that a book buyer can purchase, merchandise or distribute every month. The pie is only so big and, in this industry, booksellers and book buyers unconsciously try to break the pie up in such a way that everyone gets a similar-sized piece every season. In this system a list of titles could bring in big numbers for a large publisher based on the company's overall size, but the same list, if introduced by a smaller publisher, would more than likely result in smaller numbers.

Every house looks at its seasonal list and has to set priorities. The "90/10 Rule" plays a major role in the placement of titles. The rule says that 90% of the overall buy comes from 10% of the titles. If you are an author whose book falls outside that 10%, then you have an uphill battle and need as much information as possible to make yourself and your book standout from the rest of the titles on the seasonal list.

In-House Distribution

For an editor, part of the job is to distribute the manuscript of new books in-house. If the book is being crashed (added to a current seasonal list), this can be a good thing. However, if the title is scheduled many months in the future, the manuscript may get lost in the piles of other manuscripts, reading copies and galleys constantly being distributed around publishing houses. Usually a manuscript will get this type of early distribution only if an editor is trying to make a statement in-house about the new author or is positioning herself against other editors. If an editor has a reputation for paying large advances or always sending out manuscripts when signing a new author, this can be a "kid-who-cried-wolf" story and rarely will the manuscript be given any importance, let alone read.

One important aspect of preparing for the new season is determining which titles will have reading (and/or galley) copies made available to everyone in-house and which will have these materials provided to booksellers. Galley copies and especially reading copies are expensive to print and are often a strong indicator of how important a title is to the company. By making reading copies available, publishers are trying to convince book buyers that they support a book.

Just to clarify, a manuscript is a copy of the actual typed pages of an author's writing, usually reproduced exactly as the pages were submitted to the editor, without editorial corrections. Galley copies are manuscripts that may or may not be edited, then formatted for printing and given a plain soft cover for advance reading purposes only. Reading copies have been edited, the pages typeset for printing and bound in the actual jacket used for publication. Galley and reading copies are not for resale.

The scheduling of any new list of titles, including the accumulation of materials to be distributed to the salespeople at a future conference, is a major task. Making sure everything is completed on schedule and keeping the best interest of each title in mind is a daunting assignment. It requires teamwork and usually the process runs smoothly. With so many titles, so many covers and so much advertising and publicity, you can see how certain titles will get lots of attention, while most will not. If you are a new author with a new book and you have no idea of how the process works or how to develop relationships in-house, your chances of getting the attention your book needs to succeed are slim. Learn the basics of the business and you will improve your chances tremendously.

Positioning on the List

Where your book is positioned on a seasonal list is not as important as making certain that the assortment of budget numbers assigned to your book are appropriate for the category with the goal of achieving a high sell-through. Positioning simply indicates where your book is being presented in the catalog. If you are the author of a category book, such as a mystery or science fiction, your publisher will undoubtedly have several books from the same category being published the same month as your own. There will be one title positioned first, ahead of all the other titles from the same category, if there are five titles, each will be slotted in positions one through five.

Again, the importance here is the number assigned to your book not the position on the list. The higher the position, the higher the number assigned to your book and the higher the expectations. Position should only be important to you if you are looking to make a big splash in the marketplace, which does not always translate into net sales. You need to concern yourself with building sales, creating a good sales history with a high sell-through. The only way to do this is to focus on where your book is being distributed, in what numbers and how you as an author can generate publicity to help sell your book.

THE IMPORTANCE OF BUDGETS

To be a successfully published author in today's environment, you must have a basic understanding of the numbers and what they mean and how they are developed. Successful authors are ones whose books sell more net copies than are returned. This is a simple principle: if your publisher prints 100 copies, the retail booksellers need to sell at least 60 and return only 40. How you get to the 100 and the 60 are the most important parts of that equation. The only way to fully understand the entire process of sales and distribution is to understand the numbers, how they are created and the potential problems.

To Each Title a Number

Every title published has a number assigned to it, just as an ISBN or category is assigned to every book. It is important to know what that number represents and what affect it has on your book. In-house, the most important is called the budget number. The budget number represents the total number of copies the company needs to distribute or ship on any book—not sell, but ship. Sometimes there are two budget numbers: the preliminary number, which is determined to be a realistic idea of what the book can *reasonably* expect to sell net at retail; and the *real* budget, which is the number assigned to the book that everything in-house is based upon. Here I will focus on the real budget number.

Authors need a high sell-through on every book. The sell-through percentage is the number of total net copies that sell as a percent of the total number printed and shipped. This number is meaningless until the book has had several months of publication life. This time allows the title plenty of opportunity to work its way through the system, because eventually some copies will end up as returns. For example, a book with a print order of 10,000 total copies that sells 6,000 at the retail end will have a sell-through percentage of 60%. Six months after first publication is when you will get a more accurate sell-through percentage. This is when you should expect the 60% just mentioned. In the first month after publication that sell-through percentage will probably be 95%, because the book has not had time to work its way through the system from publisher to bookseller to retail and, eventually, back to publisher as a return.

Where It Starts

The budget numbers is the cornerstone of everything the publisher does and is the only number, bottom line, felt relevant to the company. Sales departments develop budget numbers on a calendar basis. Beginning in late summer and early fall each book on each seasonal list for the next calendar year must be given a budget number.

This represents what the company must have as a minimum number of copies ordered and distributed to customers around the country. Within the department this is often referred to as "what is needed out the door." This budget number is what the company uses when they discuss titles at meetings. Prior to publication, the sales group rarely, if ever, uses any number other than the real budget numbers.

Before this budget process begins, several of the top sales managers will have attended meetings where publication schedules of titles and preliminary budget numbers were discussed, so they bring some understanding of the company's needs and expectations for each title. This eliminates any confusion as to what the sales department *considers* possible to move out the door versus what the company says they *must* get out the door.

Furthermore, publishers will also have given each title a number indicating the total copies needed to ship for the book to be profitable. All of this was taken into consideration when the seasonal list of titles was laid out and scheduled for publication. Now it is the sales department's turn to come up with their budget numbers. Ideally, the sales budgets should match, or even exceed, what the company needs to make money on each book. However, in my experience, this rarely happens.

The Process Begins

When the sales department begins the process of developing the budget, they have little else to go on other than a title, a category and the author's name. It is not unusual for many of the titles to not have a cover, price, fact sheet (which gives the staff a summary of the plot), author information or sales history. If the publication month or "pub month" is far enough out in the schedule, a title will be positioned in one slot on the list and by the time the pub month rolls around, the book may have been repositioned to a lower spot. This happens because the company works so far in advance of the publication date that new books bought in the meantime might result in repositioning of earlier titles.

Despite the lack of basic information, the department is rarely given a chance to go back and revise the budget on a title in relation to its new positioning. They have to live with what was first proposed to corporate. This is a problem especially if a title is budgeted at a top slot and then drops to a lower position when a "bigger" book and author is acquired. This is one of the ways the budget process breaks down. The company needs the number first budgeted, but the book either doesn't deserve it or can't handle the number based on the new lower position on the list. The result can be failure for the title.

When the budget was originally researched and preliminary numbers assigned, all factors were taken into consideration and a realistic budget was given to a title. If, for example, the earlier number was 1000 and the budget needed to be revised, that number could increase to 1500 or even 2000, creating an unreasonable expectation for the book. The sales history or category track record did not suddenly improve, only the budget number was raised, illustrating what the company expects to sell and distribute to an already shrinking marketplace.

The result, in this scenario, will be excessive distribution on titles that will invariably end up with a poor sell-through percentage. When this happens, a book can often be looked upon, in the eyes of the company and the bookseller, as a failure. This is how numbers can have a huge effect on the career of an author and it has absolutely nothing to do with the writing, quality of the book, package, price, or anything. This is the nature of the business today and the only way to overcome this problem is to understand the process and learn how to have your suggestions heard in-house.

Factors in Determining the Budget

The month a book is scheduled for publication is important. Based on sales history, publishers have a good idea how books sell at certain times of the year. For example: diet, fitness and health titles are typically published in the early part of the year as people are preparing for summer. More gift books are published in the fall prior to the holiday season. New authors are not usually launched during the fall period because that is the publication time for many of the big-name authors and a wide assortment of gift related titles. These are only general rules, but true for most trade publishers.

Positioning on the list means at what slot a book is placed. Each season the list has titles at the top of each pub month, the top tier of titles being the ones in which the company has the highest expectations and the largest budget numbers. These are the titles that create the largest orders, which in turn create the largest amount of billing for the publisher. These are also the titles that get the most attention from the company and the largest amount of resources are devoted to their merchandising and marketing. There can be any number of titles on a monthly list, the lower the position or slot the smaller the budget and the lower the expectations.

Category is important because book buyers only purchase a limited number of titles within certain categories. This corresponds to their overall budget for purchases based on cover prices and other factors. Fiction is the largest category, so retailers only purchase a set number of titles for any given month. That number will far exceed what they buy for their science fiction category and typically more than they buy for their nonfiction category. This is why the category designation for a book is important when setting budgets; there is a realistic expectation of what booksellers will buy from particular categories of books.

Company Expectations

Company expectations are the single most important factor when setting budget numbers. This is what the house needs to meet their financial projections and of course make money on a book. The expectations for a title are set when the book is acquired and is the basis for the profit and loss statement the editor and finance department puts together when the publisher meets to discuss the possible purchase of the rights to that title. However, often the reality of the marketplace does not always match these expectations and this is part of the continual breakdown of the entire budget process.

The sales and marketing departments within the major trade publishing houses have the ability to generate an enormous amount of detailed sales reports. They can outline sales by day, week or month and compare them to at least the past three years and sometimes beyond. These sales can be broken down by the title of the book, the author, category or class of customer, meaning chain bookstores versus independent bookstores, distributors or book jobbers. When budgets are developed, the sales group depends on these detailed reports to give them a sales history of authors and categories.

Presenting Budgets to Corporate

At the end of the budget process, after the sales department has researched and established workable budget numbers they feel are realistic, the numbers must be presented to corporate. Inevitably, sales, editorial, finance and executive management numbers will not match or even come close. So, after the sales staff has worked for weeks putting together what they feel are realistic budgets based on their knowledge of their customers and the marketplace, they are told they need to go back and revise the numbers.

This is where the process continues to break down, because now budgets are being given to books that have no reasonable chance of making the expected number. When this happens, the list of titles usually does not change. The sales group is asked to revise the budget upward on the same list of books. For example, if the total projected gross billing—based on the budget numbers—totals $50 million and corporate sends it back saying they need $60 million, the original list of titles has not been altered and nothing has been added. This means the additional $10 million has to be increased across the board on virtually all titles. How does the sales department squeeze an additional $10 million out of an existing list of titles? They raise the budget number on as many titles as they possibly can.

Once the finance people compare the budgets developed by the sales department with the expectations of the editors (which were the basis for what was paid for a book), reality sets in. The company bought the book based on information the editor provided at the acquisitions meeting. Often, months later, everyone finds out the information was a bit skewed or was even blatantly inaccurate. The sales team might then decide the book does not deserve the budget number the company wants. Then corporate will most likely tell the sales group the new number is unacceptable and they must find a way to increase the budget. In the end, because the company may have paid too much for a book, the sales department is forced to get out larger numbers than the book deserves. If the book then fails, and returns come back heavy, money is lost and the process continues.

Mature Market

Publishing is a mature market and not a growth business, so the sales team has limited options for increasing numbers. Their task is to figure out how the company can hit all its budget numbers, meet company expectations and grow by a certain percent the next year based on the titles the company has on the seasonal list. This means refiguring the numbers, which can mean excessive distribution, which results in heavier than necessary returns, which is bad for the booksellers and even worse for the authors. Trying to find solutions to these problems happens every day and is not an easy task.

Every major trade publisher is faced with this same problem in one way or another. Sales executives sit down and take a close look at the publication schedule and the budgeted numbers, perhaps with some competitive information, and try to make decisions on the individual titles which they feel have a reasonable chance to grow based on all the intangibles. If the sale handles (sound bites for a book) are not strong enough to support a given budget number, then the sales department needs to come up with some new handles they feel can be explained to a buyer without causing too much embarrassment or loss of credibility.

In the business of publishing, the word *grow* should not be confused with Webster's definition of grow, but should be looked at as another way of saying, "increase the numbers out the door." Sales executives make recommendations—such as changing certain titles to different months—in hopes of capitalizing on some obscure point that might get them leverage with book buyers or enable them to ask the company for additional promotional support. Sometimes they ask to extend an author's tour or create a new tour. But, of course, these things cost money.

Publishers, like any other company, have spending budgets for advertising, publicity and promotion. When the sales department asks for additional money for a title in a vain attempt to meet a budgeted number, the request will likely be followed by the question, "Will this increase the number out the door?" Usually, the additional funding will improve the chances of hitting the original number, not increase that number. So how does the sales team hit the budget numbers, increase the distribution and grow the business without spending money for additional advertising or promotion? They over-sell and over-distribute. It seems to become a game and the losers are the authors who have worked so hard to write a book, only to find their creations are being used like pawns in a round of "How to Hit the Number."

Questions to Ask

If your book is on the upcoming seasonal list, there will be a sales conference where the entire department is given final preparation for their upcoming presentations to book buyers. Budgets have been set far in advance of this meeting and the goal is for everyone to leave the sales conference with a clear understanding of what they must sell to meet budget in their territories and to their individual bookselling customers. If you do not understand what has happened up to this point in your book's publication life, then you are at a tremendous disadvantage. From this point forward, even though your book has not been sold, critical details surrounding its publication have been set and will rarely be changed.

As you learn more and begin to develop an understanding of how budget numbers are set, you place yourself in a situation where you can have a positive impact. More than likely, the budget will have no relationship to what the company expects in net sales of your book. Once you develop a good working relationship with the sales and marketing department, you can ask the following questions: What is the budget on my book? How did you arrive at the budget number? How many copies do you expect to ship? How many copies do you expect to sell? With the answers, you can hopefully make some kind of determination about whether the information you are getting sounds true, based on what you have read here.

Settling on a Budget

Eventually the budget for the upcoming year is put to bed and the company now has time to catch up with current titles on sale, the current month being sold and preparation for the next sales conference. Those books far out in the pub schedule have just been given a budget and now they become dormant for a period of months. They are rarely thought about, let alone talked about, until their season rolls around and they are scheduled for presentation at a sales conference.

When preparation for the next publishing season begins in earnest, the book will finally come to the front of everyone's attention. All sales-related material will get distributed in-house and to the salespeople around the country. Most often, all marketing material will be available for the sales conference. If the manuscript was circulated when the book was sold, those who read it will have either favorable or unfavorable memories of what they read. If those memories were unfavorable, the hill gets a little steeper.

The budget numbers are what the publisher uses to make projections for the next calendar year. In the corporate world of the mega-media and entertainment conglomerates, every division or department makes projections. Later on during the course of the year each division is asked to reforecast their numbers. Since the original projections from the publishing division are always pie in the sky, the numbers have to be reforecast, which means downward, as sales and budgets come in below expectations. It is a dance done every year but even a reforecast will not prevent the over-distribution problem that plagues the industry

How the Process Can Affect Your Career

Let's say you have written two books and both have moderate sales of around 10,000 net copies each. Suppose the number of copies distributed on each was around 15,000. This represents a sell-through percentage of 66%, which is good. The third book is scheduled for publication and, since the author's first two books have performed well, the sales group decides to set a new budget of 20,000. However, the company will look at this title as one that can easily be revised upward because they need to show growth, and so the new budget is 30,000 copies. What happens?

Depending on where this book is positioned on the list and the other comparable titles positioned in the months before and after, the sales team has to make a decision. The first question would be: why 30,000 as a budget? What sets this book apart? Typically, the answer will be that the author now has three books and the company wants to show growth on title number three. The only way to achieve that is by distributing more copies.

Buyers, of course, are wary and the salespeople are reluctant, but the decision is made to set the budget at 30,000. Now the sales department feels a certain amount of pressure to increase the number out the door. This is how books get over-distributed, resulting in a poor sell-through percentage, which damages the author's chances of growing their net sales at retail.

If the company is successful in getting out the additional 10,000 copies and the third one sells a net of 15,000, which is a 50% increase over the first two books, the company will see 15,000 copies coming back in returns and the sell-through will drop from a healthy 66% to a respectable 50%, a downward turn that will not go unnoticed by book buyers. Now, multiply this scenario by 50 or 100 titles a season and you can see the result. This is how bad decisions are made and how the sell-through percentage of a book is damaged in the attempt to hit the numbers and force copies out the door.

THREE SEASONS

During the course of my twenty-plus years in the business I estimate I have spent at least two-and-a-half years of my life at hotels and resorts attending sales conferences, and in meetings preparing for those sales conferences. For the publisher, the sales conference is critical to the company's success because this is the point where every salesperson around the country is exposed to all the titles on the seasonal publication list they will be selling for the upcoming season. There is a tremendous amount of planning and preparation that goes into this showcase for the upcoming new seasonal titles.

The List

Each year publishers sell their titles on what is called a "list." This is sold every "season." During each calendar year there are typically three seasons. The publisher's "list" is exactly that, a list of titles sold to booksellers. When you hear the word "list" or "season" you know the conversation is about a title or group of titles on a particular seasonal list.

To coincide with each new season, the publishers hold a sales conference, usually away from the New York office. This is where they present the new list to all sales personnel and staff in preparation for the new publishing season. Sales representatives from around the country, as well as the national account people responsible for the largest booksellers, assemble to discuss anything and everything related to sales and new seasonal titles.

There are many presentations and meetings over seven to ten days. Virtually every meeting and every discussion is devoted to titles, potential problems and what has to be done to achieve the budget numbers. Each conference is opened with a speech from the CEO explaining where the company is year-to-date in terms of meeting budget and what has to be done to meet targets and goals for the rest of the year. Following this introduction, the conference begins in earnest.

Pre-Sales

Prior to each sales conference the company holds a pre-sales meeting, which is a way of preparing the sales managers for the sales conference. There are also scheduled meetings to prepare for the pre-sales meetings; these have been referred to as the pre-pre-sales meetings. Publishing can be an endless stream of pre-meetings that prepare everyone for the next round of meetings. No stone is left unturned in preparing the staff and sales group for the sale of the new seasonal list of titles. The sales conference, and preparation that goes into it, is critical to the company's success of meeting budget. This preparation seems endless and once it is over everyone connected quickly begins preparing for the next season because the list of titles never ends and the books keep coming.

The total number of titles on the publication schedule for a season can reach several hundred. Preparing to sell a list of titles means discussing each book, any possible objections a book buyer might have and the budget numbers the company wants on each title. All of this information is listed on budget and new title sheets. Most of the time is spent on those titles that have the greatest impact on the numbers. However, there are those titles that get plenty of discussion time, titles that have the potential to reach new sales levels, such as titles from relatively unknown authors or books that are targeted for special high levels of distribution.

Previewing the List

The objective of the conference is for the publishers, their editors and, usually, the national account sales people to present seasonal titles to the entire sales group in order to prepare them to sell these books to individual booksellers. The sales reps get a brief overview of the story of each book, but the conference is mainly about presenting sales handles, the "sound bites" sales reps use when selling books to a book buyer. These short quick blurbs are what the group feels is necessary to get the book buyers attention and meet the budget objectives.

The largest booksellers will have seen a preview of the new seasonal list prior to each sales conference. Regardless of the size of the bookseller, buyers are often on the same wavelength and their objections are often the same. This is used as a way to gauge their reaction, record their objections, then review and develop possible solutions. This information is then taken to the sales conference where it can be discussed, evaluated and decisions made as to how the entire sales group overcomes these objections. Once management determines how best to position the title to overcome the potential problems, the list is then presented again to the key booksellers where the national account person will ask for the order.

Sometimes one or more authors are invited to address the group at an evening dinner or luncheon event during the conference. This gives everyone a chance to meet an author and gives the author an opportunity to discuss his or her book on an individual level with people from various parts of the country. An invitation to speak at a publisher sales conference is an important opportunity for an author to meet those individuals who work behind the scenes to make things happen for his or her book. Unfortunately, the speaker is usually a celebrity author or a mega-best-selling author who least needs the face time, since the company is already totally committed to his or her books. Rarely do salespeople get to meet an unknown author at such a meeting.

Setting Priorities

The goal is for everyone to walk away from a sales conference with a clear understanding of the company's priorities for the upcoming season. Any concerns about titles from the sales group should be cleared up at this meeting, so everyone goes their separate ways completely prepared to sell the new seasonal list to book buyers across the country.

Sales conferences are timed several months in advance of actual on-sale dates of titles. A sales representative will begin their round of sales appointments immediately after leaving the sales conference even though the on-sale or publication dates for the titles on the seasonal list are several months away. Typically, appointments for those key meetings are made months in advance.

The major publishers sell the new seasonal list well in advance of the publication date. This gives the company ample time to make changes, especially if the decisions made at the sales conference fail to achieve the necessary budget objectives. Time flexibility is necessary, so unless a title is crashing the list, there's usually a few months between the sales presentation and the pub date. However keep in mind all of the important elements about your book will have been developed at this point and rarely, if ever, changed.

Hitting the Budget

Each new publishing season brings new opportunities and new challenges for the salespeople. The new season is a time of great anticipation. No matter how good or how bad the publication list is for a new season, the budget numbers the salespeople have to hit to meet their territorial budget are usually staggering. There is rarely a sales conference where the group doesn't walk away scratching their heads, wondering how in the world they are supposed to hit their budget numbers. The stress level starts to climb. As with most businesses today, the sales groups' bonus and annual salary increase boils down to *"What have you done for me lately?"*

I like to describe the sales conference as the company giving birth each new season to a baby monster growing at a phenomenal rate and needs to be constantly fed—a monster that never seems to sleep and only eats. For the sales reps the daily focus is on feeding that monster and that means hitting the budget numbers. The imperative seems to be: forget the strength of the titles; find a way to keep the numbers going up. Direction from the executive level is to keep the baby fed and happy, no matter what. This translates into hitting the budgets on each title and staying above the overall budget number. The resulting amount of stress in the sales department can remain at an unbearable level. Never, in my twenty-plus years in the business, did my sales group manage to meet or exceed budget on each and every title of a new publishing season, and never on the overall budget.

After the sales conference the sales people spread out across the country to meet with book buyers and sell titles. These initial meetings and the resulting orders provide feedback on which titles are hitting budget and which are not. When titles in a seasonal list are not meeting the company expectations, the individual sales reps' territory starts to fall below the budget-level objective. This typically happens after the first couple of meetings with key book buyers. Now the rep has to start scrambling to find a way to make up the budget shortfall. The bottom line— they must find alternate titles in the list to make up the difference.

Missing the Budget

It is rare that the sales rep can find another title or two in the list to take up the slack for one falling below expectations. In some cases they try to push out more copies of the biggest author's newest mega-best-selling title of the season. This is the problem that can cause a book buyer to overbuy or over-distribute certain titles and in turn, usually causes the sell-through percentage on each to drop. Most often, book buyers do this as a favor to the sales rep so the New York office won't give the rep too hard a time for not meeting the numbers. So, as you can see, the constant focus is on hitting numbers, meeting budget, feeding the monster.

Sometimes, when budget shortages become large enough, editorial is forced to start beating the bushes for another title to crash the list to make up for the shortfall. Actually, editors are constantly on the lookout for a potential new title that can be added to the current list. But when the numbers on the new seasonal list are not meeting expectations and there are no new titles at present to sell, salespeople come under pressure to increase their backlist sales, older titles that continue to sell a consistent number of copies. In all of this mayhem, the newer authors with the newer titles are often the ones who suffer most.

If the sales team doesn't have a steady stream of new titles and new product, the billing drops and revenue starts to fall. If the reps want to avoid the wrath of the top floor, they make absolutely certain the budget numbers, which represent the billing and revenue, are consistent, steady and hopefully rising.

Constant Need for New Product

Publishers are on a constant search for new product. There is always a need to bring in a new group of books. As editors search for new product, publishers are preparing their publication schedules. Titles are given final edits, production is working to prepare manuscripts for print and jackets are being created so everything will be in place for the upcoming publication season. The sales group is monitoring the budget numbers on the current set of titles now on sale, developing marketing plans for new titles and researching the sales history of titles for the next season.

The art department is constantly meeting with editors and with sales for input on the design of new covers for each of the hundreds of titles. Meanwhile, advertising is meeting with publishers from various imprints, editors and sales executives are working up copy for ads that will appear in newspapers, magazines, radio and TV across the country. Publicity is also holding meetings and working nonstop to get authors lined up for appearances on national shows and book tours. Meetings are being held to decide which titles are to be published in what month. The work is constant and the stress level is often high. All this preparation is dependent on one thing, hitting the budget numbers. That is paramount to what everyone in the company is doing. Everything depends on meeting budget.

Internal preparation for the next season, next list of titles and next sales conference begins the week after the last meeting ends. Publishing houses are constantly abuzz with activity, always making preparations for the next title or list of titles. The production of the product—the books—is constant and necessary. All the preparation that goes into each new season is focused on presenting the titles to the salespeople at the next sales conference. If the editors, publishers and national account people cannot present the sales group with a list showing how each title appears deserving of the assigned budget number, then the hopes of hitting an overall budget will be quickly dashed. The sales group has plenty of opportunity to preview each title prior to sales conference, but the actual presentation is important. These people are the ones who walk away and meet face-to-face with book buyers from around the country. I used to tell every editor and publisher involved in presenting titles at the sales conference that they must sell the sales group. They are the hardest bunch to convince, but you need to have them talking about your titles with excitement, not hesitation or reluctance.

This is the process of preparing the sales group to sell new titles; it happens three seasons a year.

THE SALE OF YOUR BOOK

Your work at to this point is now resting on the shoulders of the sales representatives and national account managers who sit in front of those book buyers and make the pitch for your book. Here are some of the problems they face, what they encounter in each appointment and how they attempt to overcome any objections.

The 90/10 Rule

Each season on every list, the top 10% of the titles get 90% of the orders (the "buy") from the bookseller and, of course, this represents 90% of the billing. The rest of the titles on the seasonal list can be subject to negotiation between the sales representative and the book buyer. Before each appointment the sales rep will ask themselves: Which of the titles do I need to get numbers and which ones can I allow the buyer to pass? The answers that were set in stone after the sales conference are now up to a small amount of interpretation, because each bookseller and book buyer is different. So the way in which the rep presents titles and in what order can make a big difference in the buy of an individual title and the overall sale.

As the reps evaluate the seasonal list and compare it to the competition, the book buyer is attempting to answer one question: Which of these titles do I need to have in my store for my customers and which ones can I forego? Passing on a title happens all the time, every day and with a lot of books. If you happen to be the author of one of these books and you hope to support yourself and your family by writing, then you need to know that all of the work you have put into your book can be gone in an instant if enough book buyers pass on your book, because then your title continues to drop down the list regardless of its position. The sales group begins to lose confidence and with each successive appointment will put forth less effort in attempting to achieve numbers on that particular title. It then becomes one of those books where the book buyer can pass without so much as a whimper of objection from the sales representative.

Focus Titles

Salespeople have to concentrate on the "focus titles" each season, those top 10% that have the highest expectations and require the full support and backing of the publisher. These are the titles that would have been laid out and discussed at length during the sales conference. These priority titles are the ones sales reps know will get the most attention from management. The sales rep's objective with each appointment is to hit the budget number on those focus titles, beyond that are the 90% of the titles that represent less than 10% of the total billing.

When a title is the third or fourth book from a particular author and the earlier titles have sold several hundred net copies on an initial purchase of a thousand, the bookseller will most likely buy one thousand. The only way out of that rut is if the publisher decides it's time for a bump up the budget-number ladder. Ideally, there is justification for the increase, aside from the fact the company needs the higher number. So when the sales rep presents that title to the book buyer who knows the third or fourth book by this author has sold a consistent net number, the buyer will hardly flinch when the sales rep tells him the higher number she wants him to buy, as long as it is fits into the previous sales pattern.

Salespeople may separate out the titles they like personally. Often they can choose the ones that have local significance such as those whose plot is based locally or whose author was born or raised or went to school in the state—anything to gain an edge. Reps are also well aware of with which titles the company feels a need to show growth; again, these are usually the top 10%. The remaining 90% of the list are the ones that require special skills to sell. This is where sales reps try to capitalize on their relationship with a book buyer to gain advantage while remaining honest and candid. Their task is a difficult one.

The Rest of the List

For the non-priority 90% of the seasonal list of titles, salespeople desperately need an edge, a good sales handle, "sound bite", or any kind of helpful details to make a successful sale. Remember, a certain amount of negotiation goes on every season and some titles are traded for others. When the salespeople need some sort of buy on an individual title, they will do whatever they can to avoid the big zero.

Publishing—and especially the sale—are all about the sales numbers or sales history and how they are interpreted. Skilled salespeople can make numbers look good to anyone other than those with an experienced eye. For an author, proper distribution and sales at the retail level are the keys to being published successfully. Suppose, for example, your publisher told you they were printing 25,000 copies of your new book. Your agent tells you that's a wonderful number for a first book. How do you know it's a wonderful number?

Remember, the marketplace is only so big and there are only so many titles that can be bought and distributed across the country. That pie can be sliced into only so many pieces. It is not getting bigger and the marketplace is not growing. If anything, it is shrinking. So the big question for the author is: What is a good number for my book? I would be willing to guarantee that your agent will not know and more than likely your editor will not know, but you can bet the sales department knows.

Proper Distribution

Getting the proper distribution for your book is vitally important. That means the right quantities to the right customers, with distribution to the right places. Your publisher might be printing the right number, but distributing to the wrong places. If that is the case, it can spell disaster for you and your book.

Booksellers are guaranteed a sale, which means they can return books at anytime and be given full credit. So how do you avoid returns? How do you increase your net copy sales? The answers lie in the distribution and the numbers, which are the basis of what the sales representatives and national account people are attempting to do every time they make a presentation of a seasonal list to a book buyer.

Publishers want to reduce returns, not eliminate them. They want to keep them as low as reasonably possible. Trying to eliminate returns means you run the risk of under-distributing a book. Considering the current philosophy of publishing companies, this can be just as bad as over-distributing. A higher than usual sell-through percentage means the book has missed sales through under-distribution. What any good publisher wants to do is reach that optimum level of sales to returns. This level can vary depending on the category and title.

Most publishers in today's climate have a sales philosophy of gross over net. This means you get as many copies shipped as possible and don't worry about the net sale. Especially during tough times when companies are having trouble making their numbers, gross over net will be the order of the day. There was a time when salespeople around the country sold a new season of titles with the only goal being the net sale of a book. As times changed and sales have become harder to come by, companies have shifted to a goal of getting the most numbers out with the hope the titles will sell through. This is a gross over net philosophy.

An author whose numbers are going up with each book while the sell-through percentage is dropping is in trouble. If this is your situation, your career as a writer is in jeopardy. Remember, salespeople can make numbers look good to the untrained eye. They can send you all the documentation in the world to explain why your net percentage is going down, but if you are serious about your craft and want to continue writing under your current name, then you need to put a stop to the drop in your book's sell-through.

There are many ways to do this and as an author you have to make some hard decisions and start asking some really tough questions. It would be hard to expect a straight answer from the in-house folks. I do not mean to suggest there are not plenty of really good, honest, hard-working employees at publishing houses, but any time an author wants to discuss the numbers assigned to her book, alarm bells go off. When alarm bells go off, in-house people can be masters at covering their butts. After all, they deal with a lot of agents and authors, most of whom have an agenda.

The preparation pays off when the rep is sitting in front of a book buyer and is successful in receiving a purchase order for the budget number they want and need.

The rest is up in the air. As an author, especially if your title is not in the top 10% of the list, you want to separate yourself and your book from the other 90%. This way you give the sales group the edge they desperately need to get an order. Little things make a difference, but it all boils down to the sale.

Distribution is the process of getting your book into the hands of booksellers. This is important and bears repeating. If you want to continue your career as an author, you want to get the right quantity into the hands of the right bookseller to maximize the net sale. The wrong quantity shipped to the wrong bookseller can result in excessive returns that lower your net sale. The lower the net sale on your book(s), the greater the chance your career as a writer will be cut short. Understanding distribution is a key part in your future as a successfully published author.

Knowing to which bookseller your book is being sent and in what quantity is essential to maximizing the net sale. The development of numbers and their relationship to distribution is an all-important part of the publishing business. The more you know, the better your chances of improving your net sale and securing your future as a successfully published author.

Finally Your Book Goes On-Sale

This is the point where it all comes together; your book is ready for shipment. Once that title arrives at its destination it will either be placed on retail store shelves for sale or resold by the jobber or warehouse. Selling books is difficult. To separate your title from the thousands on the market is an arduous task, at best. There are never any guarantees; however, with the proper mix of distribution, focused marketing and an aggressive publicity campaign, you have as good a chance as any to have a successful sale of your book. Successful means selling more net copies at retail than are returned. High sell-through is your goal and without it your career may be over before it has a chance to get off the ground.

Part 3

THE MARKETING OF BOOKS

Marketing is critical to the sale of your book and can be your key to becoming a successful author. Whether you are self-published, with a small press, or contracted to a big New York publisher, marketing to readers is competitive. Here you will discover how the major publishers market their product, which will provide you with insight into what you can do to be competitive and how to take advantage of their weaknesses.

If you do not learn how to market and make decisions about marketing, your chances of making valuable suggestions to your publisher are limited. Your book is the accumulation of years of hard work finally packaged and offered for sale to the reading public. You must understand your competition and how you can improve your chances of selling copies. The most talented writers in the world will not be successful unless the marketing of their book is focused on a specifically targeted market.

The person standing on a street corner holding a placard is marketing. Those annoying little signs you see staked at busy intersections announcing a new product or service is marketing. Junk mail enticing you to subscribe to a newspaper, newsletter or magazine is marketing. Newspaper articles written about authors and their books are a part of marketing, too. There are many forms of marketing, some simple or complex and some free and expensive; however, the important point to remember is that every book is different. There is no set formula you can plug a book into and presto, it's marketed. Successful books have a good marketing plan behind them and here we will take a look at how those plans are developed.

Consumers and Customers

With the dramatic change in the business of trade book publishing over the past fifteen years, the focus of their marketing has shifted to adapt to those changes. No longer is marketing geared solely toward luring the individual reader or consumer into retail locations to buy books. Now the marketing efforts are focused in two areas. The first is directly to the bookseller, the customer to whom the publishers sell their product, to entice them to buy larger quantities of books. The second is to the individual reader (or consumer), the ultimate purchaser of the product, to convince them to buy books at the retail bookseller.

The distinction between the consumer (reader) and the customer (bookseller) is important. When reference is made to the consumer, this is the person who goes into a retail bookseller and buys a book; they are the ultimate purchaser of the product. The customer is the company the publisher sells books to directly; whether they're a retailer, wholesaler or distributor, they buy the books from the publisher and are referred to as booksellers. Keep the difference in mind as you read ahead.

Marketing directly to the booksellers has become more important as the business has changed. There has always been a marketing effort aimed at the book buyer who makes the purchasing decisions for the company and to whom the publishers directly sell books, but the focus on, and resources given to, the bookseller have increased substantially. There has always been and will always be national television, radio or print campaigns aimed at the consumer. However, the length to which publishers will entice book buyers has gained prominence over the past decade.

Advertising

In marketing there are three major areas of focus: Advertising, Promotion and Publicity. Advertising is the paid placement of a product in media venues. A person or company pays a fee to advertise their product on or in a particular media vehicle for a specified period of time. Commercials on television and radio, print ads in newspapers and magazines, and online banners and links are all paid placements. Advertising for a book is the least effective method of the three marketing components and by far the most expensive.

This is not to say that advertising is not effective, but the ability of publishers to quantify the impact of dollars spent to copies sold is limited. Certainly you can identify spikes in sales after a major media blitz that includes a combination of TV, radio and print advertising. However, when they attempt to examine the cost effectiveness of the money spent when compared to the increase in sales, it is nearly impossible for publishers to extrapolate.

Promotion

Promotion can best be described as anything and everything that brings attention to a product. For example: the corrugated displays you see in bookstores, or a floor, table or shelf display that attempts to separate one title from another and give it more presence in-store is considered part of a promotion. For publishers, promotions and promotional items come in two forms: first is direct-to-*consumer* (the reading public) and the second is direct-to-*customer* (the booksellers), and the latter comes in two types.

When you visit retailers and they offer anything free, such as balloons, key chains, writing pens, brochures, or make special discount or rebate offers, this is all part of the book's promotion offered direct-to-consumer, the reader.

Similarly, at major book conventions, publishers give away reading copies of upcoming new titles; they offer writing pens, badges, t-shirts, posters, any gimmick that brings focus to a particular title or group of titles. This is the first type of promotion directed at the customer. In addition to all the free stuff, publishers offer enticements or inducements to buy extra copies. This is all part of a package of promotional offers a publisher uses to meet their target of distributing or shipping a certain number of copies to the marketplace.

Publicity

Publicity is any type of free media coverage. An article about you as an author and your newly published book would be considered publicity; it did not cost you anything other than your own hard work. An interview on television or radio discussing your book would be a great form of publicity.

Anything that costs nothing more than a telephone call, letter, e-mail, or gas for your car is publicity and the most effective way to sell products.

One article with your picture in a newspaper holding your book will sell more copies than a paid advertisement in the same paper every day for a week. Consumers are much more drawn to a featured segment such as an article or interview than to an advertisement. Consumers are inundated with ads so tend to ignore the paid spots. They enjoy reading or listening to what is in essence free advertising. If you want to maximize and make your marketing dollars effective, find ways to generate publicity.

Identifying Your Market

Identifying your market is a basic principle. Books of certain price points and categories appeal to certain readers. Demographics play a role in how you market and to whom.

> **Demographics:** *The statistical characteristics of human populations, as age or income, used especially to identify markets; the demographic profile of a market such as the viewers of a TV show or readers of books (Merriam Webster).*

For books, a lot of common sense goes a long way.

As a general characterization, romance novels would not appeal to most men and as a result you would not market to men. Non-fiction titles on hunting or fishing would not necessarily appeal to women so you would not market to women. Low price point books appeal to a book retailer in an area of middle-income homes where you would find a concentration of discount outlets. Higher price point books appeal to upscale neighborhoods where you are likely to find gourmet food and wine shops. All are broad generalizations used to identify a market.

Publishers have limited marketing budgets and must maximize the dollars they spend by making certain they get the biggest bang for their buck. The same would hold true for the individual who is self-published and certainly for the small press. Identifying to whom your book would appeal and then focusing your marketing to that demographic is the only way to maximize the dollars you have in your marketing budget.

Destination or Impulse

Book retailers are either destination or impulse markets. Your local bookstore would be considered a destination market. Consumers are going to walk into that store with the idea of buying a book. The bookstore is their destination. An impulse market is one in which the primary reason for a consumer to visit is something other than buying a book, such as your local supermarket, drug store, mass merchant or price club. These locations are typically an impulse market where books are designed to catch the consumer's attention, creating an impulse sale.

Bookstores offer impulse items for purchase as well, those small displays around the store and at each cash register are impulse items. Any product that has a low price point can be considered an impulse item. The hope is that the consumer will add the item to their other purchases to increase the total sale.

Price Point and Category

The price point and category of a book are simple ways of identifying a market. Mass market paperbacks that carry a retail price of $7.99 or below are ideal for the impulse buyer in a supermarket, mass merchant or price club. On the flip side, books that carry a retail price around $14.99 are seldom found in those kinds of retail outlets. Category plays a part, too. A $7.99 biography may not be a good fit in an impulse market, but a $14.99 copy of a former bestseller with a tie-in to a major motion picture might be the perfect candidate. These are broad generalizations used as simple examples of identifying markets. Again, common sense is one way publishers market books.

HOW THE MAJOR PUBLISHERS MARKET BOOKS

Major New York trade publishers have a particular idea about how to market and to whom. They tend to follow a simple formula that includes portions of advertising, promotion and publicity and follow the same pattern to varying degrees on every successive book. Seldom, if ever, do they venture their marketing efforts outside of those parameters. Marketing to groups or individuals outside of those existing boundaries seldom, if ever, exists.

For example, publishers have an existing relationship with their recognized customers: major bookstore chains, mass merchants, price clubs, independent bookstores, supermarkets, drug stores, airports and the military. They have a recognized system for buying product, discounts are standardized, distribution is guaranteed and so the process of selling product is easy. Introduce, for example, a chain of Christian booksellers to whom trade publishers have never sold books and panic can set in at the house. Publishers do not want to consummate that sale simply because the Christian booksellers are not within their recognized and comfortable parameters. They would prefer to make that sale through a recognized customer acting as a middleman.

Push or Pull

The marketing focus has shifted from how many copies can be sold, net at retail, to how many copies can be shipped or billed to booksellers, and how much revenue can be generated. Do not confuse revenue with net sales; revenue is the total sum of the company's billing of books and does not reflect how many units will actually be sold at retail. Finding ways to generate excessive billing without regard to returns is the path the major publishers have decided to follow and is where their marketing efforts are focused.

Marketing used to be about the net sale and the goal was to pull the consumer into the retail store. That is no longer the objective of a publisher's marketing efforts. Today that goal is to push product and find ways to ship more books to each bookseller. High returns are considered part of the cost of doing business. This huge shift in focus has created enormous problems at every stage along the distribution chain, and as an author it can have a huge impact on the ability of your book to sell more copies than are returned.

The Traditional Marketplace

Little consideration is given to any market outside those recognized booksellers above that provide the distribution and warehousing of the product. This is an important fact to consider when you begin to create marketing plans for your individual book. There has been little effort made to sell directly to the consumer and none to small groups or organizations. If the order does not generate thousands of copies, then the marketing effort is barely on the radar of the largest publishers and little, if any, effort will be made.

This is a huge weakness of the major publishers and one area that can be exploited by the self-published writer and small press. However, keep in mind the traditional book marketplace is competitive and difficult to penetrate. To use a worn out phase, you have to think outside the box. For example, if you are writing a children's book where the main character is an animal, why not try to focus some of your marketing to consumers of pet stores? This is the kind of retailer that may not sell books as a rule; however, they might be tempted if the offer is good enough. It is definitely the kind of venue well beyond the traditional marketplace where major publishers are comfortable.

Marketing by Book Format

Marketing, whether to the consumer or bookseller, is different for every book format: whether it be hardcover, mass market, trade paper or juvenile. Typically, the hardcovers get the most attention, followed by the mass market paperbacks, then trade paper and finally the juvenile books. The hardcover sales generate the largest chunk of billing, which is why they get the most time and money. If you follow that logic, the mass market generates the second largest piece of billing, followed by trade paper and juvenile. This gives you some idea about the balancing of time, people and money in-house.

If you are writing a mass market paperback, you cannot expect the same kind of resources to be directed to your book, as would a hardcover title. This especially goes for writers of juvenile books at the bottom of the food chain. Original trade paperback books, those over-sized soft cover titles, though growing in popularity, get some attention and resources, but certainly not as much as the two formats that precede them. The reason is billing. The format that generates the most billing gets the most attention and available resources. Rarely are there exceptions to this rule, but I've learned to never say never!

Discounts

The discount at which publishers sell books to their customers cannot be based on volume. It's a law designed to balance the playing field. The price at which the largest chain bookstore in the country buys a hardcover is the same as the single local independent bookstore no matter how many they order. The same holds true whether the book is a mass market paperback, trade paperback or juvenile title. The discount cannot be based on volume. Discounts for class of trade, such as a wholesaler or book retailer can be different, but not based on the size of the business or volume of their total purchases.

For example, hardcover books will have one discount, mass market and trade paperbacks another discount and juvenile books a third discount. Retailers do not buy the book from a publisher at the same discount or price as the wholesaler or distributor because the wholesaler or distributor is the middleman in the distribution chain and will ultimately resell the book to a retail bookseller. The discount schedule will change depending on whether the bookseller is a retailer, wholesaler, distributor or book jobber.

Incentives

Because publishers cannot legally sell books at prices based on volume, they circumvent the restriction in a number of creative ways. Publishers will offer a variety of incentives to their customers and these incentives are paid based on volume. For example, they may offer a book in a floor display and will pay their customer $5 per display ordered. The local independent bookstore might buy one floor display and for that purchase receive a payment (typically through a credit issued to the invoice) of $5 called a placement allowance.

For the large chain, which might operate over a thousand stores, they too are eligible and as a result may buy more floor displays than they have actual stores and receive a $5 placement allowance for each purchase. Considering the national chain has the capacity to order much larger quantities the payment is obviously much larger. If you multiply this example times several books per publisher you can see how the discount restriction based on volume is easily circumvented and puts the small local independent bookstore at a distinct competitive disadvantage.

One way the publisher is able to use incentives to favored accounts is through the use of preset qualifying limits for a placement allowance. The small bookstore may have a limit of one display required for the $5, however if the publisher needs to force copies they will set the limit at two displays. This means the store must order at least two displays to qualify for the $5 placement fee. Typically, the small stores will pass, but not the chains. If a chain has 1500 stores, the publisher may set their qualifying limit at 2000 displays, which for the chain may end up being negotiable. Numbers like these are outside the realm of the small independent bookstore. The result is that the chain will buy what they need to get the placement allowance and worry about the returns later.

This is how the larger retailers or booksellers are able to create a nice revenue stream from the publishers without worrying about a volume discount. This is also why they end up buying more books than they should. They do not want to miss out on the opportunity to receive an extra payment for a title they would buy anyway. In the end, the system starts to break down and the individual author's sales begin to suffer.

The Goal is to Ship More Books

Publishers today are more than willing to give away discount and other incentives such as advertising allowances and promotional dollars for the opportunity to ship larger quantities of books. This is all carefully calculated to weigh the cost of these promotions versus the total distribution, billing and revenue generation. Publishers know that in order to offer a placement allowance on a floor display they must ship a certain number of displays to cover the cost. This is why it has become so critical to ship larger and larger quantities of all books to booksellers—to cover the cost of the promotional allowances.

This has a ripple effect throughout the distribution chain. First, the publisher is willing to ship more books and the bookseller, whether a retailer, distributor, wholesaler or jobber, is willing to buy more books and to accept more books into their distribution process. This forces retailers to turn their inventory quicker and create bigger returns, all in an effort to find placement for the disproportionate number of books entering the marketplace, which is a direct result of the incentives the publishers are willing to offer.

Take everything I have written up to this point, including the function of placement allowances, advertising fees and promotional fees. Consider the fact there are any number of publishers large and small all in competition for the same limited retail space using the same tactics. Multiply all publishers times hundreds of titles being published each year times the tens of thousands of dollars being offered and you begin to get some idea about the over-distribution problem and the current state of the mainstream traditional trade publishing business.

BESTSELLER LISTS

The term "bestseller" is synonymous with a book being selected for a position on a list, in any recognized print medium, located anywhere in the country. The designation of "national bestseller" means a book has been selected for a position on a list of best-selling books in a print medium that has national distribution. The selection of a book for a best-selling list does not mean that title has sold a certain number of copies; it only means the book was selected for a best-selling position relative to other books in that market.

When you see the word "bestseller" printed somewhere on the cover, or more commonly the words "national bestseller," it gives the prospective reader the feeling that the book has sold a lot of copies. Which means it must have been read by a lot of people. The flap or jacket copy makes the story sound interesting when the publisher is comparing this book to any mega-best-selling title. This designation is misleading and is part of the company's marketing effort aimed at selling that book.

If *you* had written a novel being compared to the latest #1 national bestseller, you would be ecstatic! Place the shoe on the other foot, you are now the consumer, you buy a hardcover for a bit less than $30, you get home and soon discover it reads nothing like the particular book to which it was compared. You would probably be upset, especially if the book was not a good read and certainly not worth the price you paid.

The Publisher Is Not the Brand

Since publishers are keenly aware they are not considered a brand in the minds of the consumer, that their *author* is the brand, they assume the readers will not retaliate against them, but against the author of the over-priced, non-comparable book purchased for slightly less than $30. So who can you trust? All publishers are guilty of the same over-aggressive marketing aimed at readers who buy books. The truth is, few if any of the books labeled "bestsellers" are truly best-selling books.

Why does it seem as if almost every new book published is labeled a bestseller? Because the industry today is focused on selling as many copies as possible to as many unsuspecting readers as they can. They stretch the truth as far as reasonably possible without violating the unwritten standards of the industry. If a book is selected as one of the best-selling titles by the local newspaper in Anywhere, USA and is placed on a printed list that appears in the paper, then it can be called a "bestseller."

The "national bestseller" is a bit more of a stretch, but, for example, if the newspaper in Anywhere, USA selects a title and places it on their list of best-selling books and that printed list appears in a newspaper which just happens to have subscribers in far reaches of the country, the title can now be called a "national bestseller." There was a time many years ago when the term was used only with books that appeared on the *New York Times* or *USA Today* bestseller list, but that line was erased long ago.

How to Label Your Book a Bestseller

The obvious conclusion here is that almost any book can be called a bestseller. If the author's hometown newspaper hears from the only bookstore in town that the new book is selling "pretty good," and the paper puts that in print on a list containing other titles, even though it is not described as a bestseller list, then the publisher could call the book a "bestseller." If challenged, all the publisher has to do is produce a copy of the newspaper where the title is listed. Of course, who's going to make such a challenge? Certainly not another publisher since they are *all* guilty of the same tactics.

In this example, the local bookstore may have only received four or five copies and could have sold as few as two or three, or none for that matter. The fact is the book was listed or described in a recognized print medium as selling "pretty good." Translation: The book is a bestseller. You can't just start your own newsletter and suddenly call your book a bestseller. It has to be an objective source, but the size of the source is not in question. The hometown newspaper could have a distribution of only a few hundred, as long as it is recognizable and objective.

National Bestsellers

As for the major national bestseller lists, that is a completely different story. The major chain bookstores and discount retailers all have the exact numbers of copies a book sold and was paid for through their cash registers. They can provide any publisher with information on how many copies that publisher's titles sold the previous week by title, format, price, in what region of the country and in which individual store location. However, these numbers are not always shared with the most recognizable national bestseller lists.

USA Today has become a leading national newspaper and they describe their bestseller list as a compilation of sales from a variety of sources. *USA Today* will seldom follow any other national lists in position or duration of titles on their list. They are secretive about their sources, but you can imagine it's practically the same as their competitor, which happens to reside in the heart of the New York publishing world.

The one list everyone in the industry follows closely is, of course, The New York Times Bestsellers. Here is where the publishers have learned how to influence as many of the best-selling decisions as possible. The Times also uses a variety of sources to make decisions on what books should be listed on their weekly bestseller list. These sources are chosen from independent booksellers, chain bookstores in selected cities and "other credible booksellers," to make selections. It is the policy of the Times not to reveal these sources.

Compiling Bestseller Lists

Having been directly involved with some of the largest retailers in the country for over twenty years, I can tell you the *Times* rarely used the single largest retailer in the country as a source for their weekly bestseller lists. Every publisher in New York City has found out which sources or bookstores the *Times* uses and which carry the biggest weight in helping them make bestseller distinctions.

Armed with this information, which is rotated periodically, every marketing department makes absolutely certain every source is amply supplied with the latest and best of everything about the titles for which they lobby strongly. If you were one of the sources, you would assume the publisher is sending the same material to every single bookseller, but you would be wrong. Publishers pay particularly close attention to the sources the *Times* uses for their bestseller list.

So every week the *Times* staff for the book review calls the sources and asks for a list of titles that have been selling the most copies. Would it surprise you to know that some of these sources do not use computers? There are book retailers around the country who still count inventory by hand and thus do not have actual unit sales to share.

The staff members then combine the lists, sit down around a big table in their conference room and make decisions based on the all the information from their sources. Whether they actually try to make tabulations based on actual unit sales is still unclear, but their lists are definitely distinctive and are often questioned for their validity compared to the lists of actual unit sales the publishers accumulate on a weekly basis.

How Many Copies Have To Be Sold

There is no threshold of a certain number of copies a book must sell to be called a bestseller, there never has been and I doubt there ever will be. Until all booksellers are able to supply similar information on actual unit sales, there is no reason for the *Times* to change the way they make selections. Besides, there are publishers who will always be opposed to an actual unit sales mechanism for selecting bestsellers. Such a selection process would take away their ability to use influence to impact the selections of the *Times*.

If the publisher fails to support a title adequately through the purchase of retail and/or web site space, what do you think the chances are that the book will make a bestseller list? Almost nil—which is why it is so astonishing when a small press title or an unknown author who was not supported well in an initial distribution of booksellers around the country makes the bestseller list of a major publication.

Hopefully, this description of how bestsellers are determined has not disappointed you. This is the business and when your book is published, you will have the ammunition to make certain it, too, becomes a bestseller.

STRENGTHS OF MAJOR PUBLISHERS

Marketing varies from publisher to publisher and the bigger publishing houses have advantages over their smaller competitors. There are five things major trade publishers do extremely well when it comes to marketing. These are the areas in which it is difficult, if not impossible, for smaller publishers to compete effectively. The money being spent and the economies of scale place the major trade publishers at a distinct advantage in these areas.

The Biggest Booksellers

The first thing the major publisher does well is to meet the needs and demands of the bigger booksellers. They assign a national account person to each of the largest and it becomes that account person's responsibility to not only sell books in large numbers, but to answer all questions, provide as much information as is requested, conduct quarterly business reviews, stay in constant contact and develop a relationship. In essence, that account person becomes the single most important person from that house to that customer. When you consider the market share, or percent of the total print order the big chains purchase from publishers, it is understandable why so much attention is paid to these customers.

Direct Marketing

The second thing the big trade publishers do extremely well is market directly to their biggest book buyers and booksellers. This direct marketing effort creates the opportunity for the publisher to present new and creative incentives as a way to entice companies to buy quantities of books much larger than that customer can reasonably expect to distribute and sell. The reason for this is to raise the effective discount of the customer, the profit margin at which they operate their business.

When you look at the publishers' overall marketing budget, a larger and larger percentage is being spent on incentives paid to the biggest booksellers. There is no way a self-published author or small press can compete. Depending on the title and total gross distribution, incentives may well exceed $50,000 on a single title.

National Advertisers

The third thing the major publishers do well is throw tens of thousands of dollars at national advertisers for space in their particular medium. Whether it is the major networks, cable television, national radio, major magazines and newspapers, the big publishers have the distinct advantage in dollars and budget to spend what they need to convince authors they are promoting their book properly to a nationwide audience. They also have the ability to buy multiple spots for a better price. If they recognize that a weekly national magazine is going to be one of their particular targeted advertising mediums, they will buy a large number of spots to cover many weekly editions at one time.

Advertising, whether print, television or radio, typically encompasses the major key markets such as New York, Washington, Chicago and Los Angeles. On the big revenue-generating titles, those four cities are always covered one way or another. Beyond that, publishers might throw in a few other major cities. Rarely do they go more than twelve or fifteen cities deep into any advertising plan for a particular title, and the top thirty media markets get the brunt of the dollars and activity.

Promoting Books

The fourth thing the major publishers do well is to promote books with in-store displays, spiffs and an assortment of what we called "chotchkies" (pronounced chotch-keys). The costs of these displays and chotchkies are far beyond the reach of the average publisher. Bought by the thousands, the production costs would be prohibitive for anyone outside the competitive mainstream. In addition to these freebies, publishers offer promotional dollars in the form of placement allowances, cooperative advertising allowances and an assortment of fees or dollars paid directly to the bookseller in return for their large order on a particular title or group of titles.

Corrugated displays are risky for the small press and certainly beyond the reach of the self-published because, outside of the major bookstore chains and local independent bookstores, there is no guarantee the display will get more than a couple of days of floor exposure.

Generate Publicity

The fifth thing the major publishers do extremely well is to generate publicity at a regional and national level. The competition for daytime talk show spots and primetime news magazines is fierce because, in the business of publishing, publicity—more than anything else—sells books. Through contacts developed over the years, the publicity departments have the ear of the key gatekeepers to the big shows, a resource virtually impossible for smaller publishers to obtain. The majors also have the advantage of negotiating one author for a higher profile author in an attempt to gain a spot for more than one author. They also have the ability to guarantee a major magazine an exclusive interview in exchange for a better price on an assortment of prime advertising space.

Of the five major areas that represent the strength of the biggest publishers, generating publicity is what they do best. An article in the *New York Times* book review will sell many times more copies than an advertisement in the same paper. One five-minute spot on a daytime talk show will generate sales many times over what a consistent media campaign will do. The ability of the publishers to reach out to their contacts and create buzz is where they drive the most business to the book retailers.

WEAKNESSES OF MAJOR PUBLISHERS

There are five areas where the major publishers fail in their marketing and where smaller publishers and astute authors can have a significant impact. These are where the major publishers, due to lack of time and resources, are unable focus their marketing efforts. Remember: rarely will they spend any time or money attempting to sell small quantities of books. There are rare exceptions, but as a general rule, the major trade publishers do not market to areas where the total purchase of books is limited to hundreds of copies.

Thinking Outside the Mainstream

The first weakness is never thinking outside the mainstream retail marketplace. Selling books directly to consumers—or any small group or organization—is way outside the thinking of the majors. Two major publishers recently began an attempt to market directly to the consumer (reader), but this is a first. If it doesn't involve an established bookseller—whether retailer, wholesaler, distributor or jobber—the majors do not consider it a potential market for their books. As a result, they will not devote time, manpower or resources to thinking of ways to reach those markets. The example mentioned earlier, of selling to Christian booksellers, proves my point. Since that customer is outside of the traditional parameters of the publisher and is not a recognized bookseller, they will not attempt to sell directly to them. Publishers would much rather secure the order through a middleman.

Part of the problem here is the sheer size of the list of titles that require daily attention. Considering the fact my former company was publishing over 1,200 titles per year, at any one time our focus stayed on the top 100-150 titles. Those included the ones currently for sale on retail shelves, ones that were six months from publication and the ones currently being sold to book buyers.

Gathering Information on Consumers

The next area big publishers fail is in gathering pertinent information on the consumer, the actual readers of their books. The benefits of understanding the consumer are well beyond their ability to comprehend. They figure that end of the business is best left to the retailers.

The word "demographics" is not relevant in the language of the major publishers. They understand the demographic of *their* customer, the booksellers, as their primary focus. There is a feeling that the amount of information gathered on the end consumer would be overwhelming. Some major publishers are still grappling with the idea of developing a customer database with key information on the more than 8,000 book customers or booksellers with whom they deal each season. Convincing executives of the need to establish and maintain such a large amount of consumer data is difficult.

Regional or Niche Markets

The third area big publishers ignore is marketing in regional or niche markets. Publishers often publish a book and then go looking for a market. They seldom think of identifying a market and then publishing to fill that demand because it is less expensive to publish a title and ship copies then it would be to research the market for potential size. From their perspective, a relevant market has to demand copies in the thousands, preferably in the tens of thousands, not hundreds. In other words, they publish to trends in the world around us without regard to whether the market can support book sales. The market typically has to be considered national in stature to be considered at all.

Publishers know trends in culture, art, television and movies happen quickly and they want to be the first ones with a book to market. They don't have the time, resources or inclination to research the market. That trend has to reach a certain saturation or tipping point before they will take notice. Capitalizing on a regional or niche market by publishing a book targeted specifically at that small market in an effort to sell a few thousand copies is not open to the major publishers.

The Power of the Internet

The creative minds at the major publishers have not figured out how to use the Internet to their advantage and this is the fourth area where their marketing fails. The web sites of the major publishers are primarily for informational purposes and not sales. There are, of course, exceptions; one exception is making an attempt to sell directly to the public, but their success has been limited. For the most part, internet marketing means advertising on some customers' web site, not utilizing the power of their own website to market or generate sales. In the past, the sales and marketing departments were not involved with the development of information for their companies' web sites, and rarely was their advice ever asked—that should tell you exactly what the majors think of the internet for marketing.

Publishers are mostly old school. Things are done the way they have been done for the past fifty years. Publishers were slow to adopt the use of computers and they have been slow to figure out how to tap into that power. They have stepped up to the plate in terms of sales information, but not the enormous power of the internet to advertise, promote or market their product. They are using their web sites primarily to disseminate information to booksellers and to the devoted reader who wanders onto a site to find the release date of their favorite author's next book.

Ignoring Middle America

The fifth and final area where publishers' marketing fails is in Middle America. They ignore markets outside of the major media hot spots. What goes on in the heartland of the country is often ignored. Regional publishing is not in the publisher's verbiage. It boils down to resources. There is a limited amount of money and manpower, so the philosophy is to focus on both coasts and hope those efforts eventually bridge the rest of the country.

The major markets are almost always covered. Those areas include New York, Chicago, Washington and Los Angeles. Beyond that, the top twenty to thirty media cities are covered on a rotating basis. Their thinking goes like this: reaching a hundred people with a single advertisement is not as effective as reaching twenty-five people four times.

So, we touched on five areas where the publishers do a good job of marketing and five where their fail. There is a tremendous amount of time devoted to marketing at most publishing houses. The more you know and understand the better chance you will have of creating marketing plans that exploit the weaknesses of your competition and improve your chances of selling books.

BASIC FACTS ABOUT MARKETING BOOKS

When you begin to develop your marketing plan (by identifying your market and deciding how best to penetrate that market) you need to consider three important aspects of the trade publishing industry: guaranteed sale, bookseller real estate and the priority of generating revenue.

Guaranteed Sale

Publishers "guarantee" the sale of books to booksellers. They guarantee the books bought from the publisher will be accepted for return with full credit. So if a bookseller orders ten copies of a title and after a period of time sells only five, the five unsold copies are shipped back to the publisher for full credit.

For authors, it is important their publishers sell the right number of copies to the right assortment of customers so these returned books are minimized (or the sale is maximized). What really determines the success or failure of a book is not what the publisher or even the book reviewers think, but what the bookseller, and ultimately the reader, thinks. A healthy net sale at retail is what a book needs to be successful in the marketplace. This net sale is called sell-through or percent of sale and represents the net number of copies sold at retail relative to the number printed and shipped.

When titles sell through at 50% or less, meaning fewer than 50% are sold at retail within a certain period of time (typically a period of several months), it is highly unlikely booksellers will hold copies in their stores. Any new title selling less than 50% over the course of a few weeks and in some cases even a few days will be returned to the publisher. Booksellers want books that quickly sell through at a minimum of 60%, and so do the publishers.

Besides the obvious reasons, higher sell-through means lower handling costs for booksellers and quicker inventory turns, which results in better and faster cash flow. Retailers cannot afford to allow books to languish. They need to find other titles so they can maximize the investment they have in the books. The less time their personnel have to spend dealing with returns, the more time they have to work with customers and order titles that do sell through at a high percentage.

Bookseller Real Estate

When you walk into a retail bookseller and see attractive floor and table displays where books are nicely stacked with scores of unique titles, keep in mind that none of this is random. When browsing shelves you will notice some books are placed face out and others spine out. This does not happen by chance. All of these displays are designed to catch the eye of the consumer and direct them to certain titles or categories. When merchandizing books, virtually every inch of that store is considered real estate and it rents to publishers for big bucks. This is the second basic fact you need to know to understand marketing.

Publishers pay dearly for the right to place their titles on those tabletops and in those floor and shelf displays. And it isn't cheap! Retailers charge a premium depending upon the time of year and the type of promotion in which publishers want to participate. So the next time you visit your local book retailer, understand the titles you see first and in the largest displays occupy space bought and paid for. This is where the major publishers dominate the marketplace. They pay prices most small publishers cannot afford, regardless of the potential strength of the book or the reputation of the author.

Generating Revenue is Priority

The third marketing aspect important to know (and which is a recurrent theme of this book) is that publishers in today's competitive climate need to generate revenue by increasing billing, which is a direct result of shipping large quantities of books. This has become the focus of all the major publishers and is the goal of their entire marketing effort. They do this by selling and shipping as many copies as they possibly can and, in most cases, by selling more copies than their customer can reasonably resell. As I've stated, this creates an over-distribution situation, which is the model for all publishers in today's market environment.

If you are wondering why any bookseller or retailer would buy more copies than they can sell, the answer is to raise their effective discount. And since book resellers and retailers are guaranteed the sale and are often paid inducements, they keep the payment for buying an over abundance of copies and return the unsold product.

If it still doesn't make business sense, then you understand clearly the single biggest problem with publishing today. This over-distribution problem is prevalent throughout and will not be going away anytime soon. That is why it is critical for writers to understand these three basic aspects of marketing and publishing: (1) the guaranteed sale, (2) bookseller real estate and, (3) the priority of generating revenue.

SIX "P's" OF MARKETING

Product, package, price, place and promotion are five Ps universally recognized by marketers of all kinds of products and services. There are six P's to the marketing of books. PUSH has become a key component of any publishing companies marketing strategy.

Product

The product, in this case, is the manuscript you've poured your heart and soul into. Your publisher wants to maximize the sale and distribution of that product as best they can and they do this by marketing the book to their customers, the bookseller.

Depending on the position of your book on the seasonal list, it will get some sort of marketing attention. The amount will depend on whether it is a hardcover, trade paper or mass market paperback. The titles generating the most billing will get the most attention and resources. This is where your understanding of the marketplace can play a pivotal role in the marketing of your book.

Package

A key component of any book is the package. The best way to describe a package is that the presentation must fit the subject. Sort of like the Supreme Court's description of pornography: it's hard to describe, but I know it when I see it!

A category book, such as mystery, romance or science fiction, needs to have a cover that clearly and easily identifies the subject. The same holds true for a biography, cookbook or business book. The cover and title should easily and quickly identify the category of a book.

Photographs versus paintings, placement of the author name and title, various colors, font size and type, are all part of what makes the package. You want something similar to other titles in the same genre or category. You do not want to stray too far from how other books of the same genre or category are packaged. If there is one thing publishers spend a lot of time deciding, it is whether or not the package is right. People in the business know it when they see it. Sometimes they get it wrong, but often the first instinct is what is important.

Price

This falls into the same realm as the package; you want to be somewhere in the middle. You do not want to be over or under priced. This holds true regardless of the format of your book. The best way to know where your book falls in the relative scale is by visiting bookstores and checking the price of your competition.

There are many factors that play a part in the price. Format and category is important. If, for instance, your book is a 125-page hardcover novella then you cannot compare the price to a 650-page biography. Hardcover books in various categories vary in their pricing. If your business book is being published in trade paper, you wouldn't want to price it several dollars above the competition, but rather somewhere in the middle of all the other trade paper business books.

However, the one exception is if you are self-published and have the ability to set your cover price. Always price it below competitive titles in the same category or genre.

Place

This term is used to reference where your book would be sold, the type of customer or bookseller. This is important because if your book were the 125-page hardcover novella, there are certain markets where the book would not be expected to sell. On the other hand, if your book is the 650-page biography, then the likelihood this book will sell in markets where the novella will not, is predictable. You should not find an expensive cookbook written by a celebrity chef in a convenience store but rather on the shelf of a high-end retail book chain where customers will easily spend $40 on a cookbook.

This goes hand in hand with the distribution. Where a book has the best chance of being sold depends on the price, category and history of previous books in the same genre. The proper placement depends on many factors, one of which concerns what is happening in complementary markets like motion pictures, television or the entertainment industry in general.

A biography of a former political or historic leader, for example, may not be appropriate for certain retailers unless there happens to be a huge marketing push going on for a new movie about the person. On the flip side, a biography of a movie star appearing in the new blockbuster may be the exact thing for the same market where the political bio was not appropriate. There are always exceptions to the general rule.

There are markets for every book, the key is finding the right one and then distributing the right quantity to maximize the sale and minimize the return.

Promotion

Think of promotion as the sauce that makes everything taste better. Promotion can be the key to a successful book.

As you read earlier, more promotional resources are aimed at the bookseller than the consumer. This is because publishers have easier and quicker access to them and can create much more of an impact with less money spent than trying to lure the consumer into a retail store.

Promotions aimed at the end consumer, the person who actually pays for the book in a retail store, can include the corrugated floor and shelf displays you see, or an overhead sign announcing a free giveaway or bookmarks, book bags, t-shirts and the like. The promotion is the method by which publishers try to catapult a title to a larger purchase than would normally be possible. Promotions are the way in which publishers maximize their initial orders on books, without regard to the potential negative impact on the sell-through. The aim is to increase the order and hopefully improve the net sale.

PUSH for Books

This premise is not a recognized part of any college marketing course but important in the world of publishing. PUSH is an important part of the overall strategy of selling books. It simply means shipping as many copies as possible to as many customers as possible to generate as much billing as possible to meet the corporate demands. PUSH is not something writers need to worry about, but something about which they should be aware.

Now you have an understanding of the five P's of traditional marketing and the sixth, PUSH, for the marketing of books.

The product is your book, for which you must choose the right package, with the correct price, and make sure it is sold to the proper places with the exact mix of promotions and not too much PUSH. Now you know the right ingredients to improve your book's chances of selling through at a high percent of sale and make yourself a successful author.

COORDINATION AND CREATIVITY

Implementing the best-laid marketing plan is meaningless unless you have product in stores. What would be worse than getting a front page article with multiple pictures of you and your book and then not have adequate copies in the hands of the retail booksellers? This spells disaster. Coordinating your distribution with publicity, in-store promotions and advertising is absolutely critical in order to maximize the sale of a book.

It is difficult, but not impossible, to coordinate publicity with on-sale dates. However, through creating a good relationship with your publisher, you can help influence advertising and promotions. The best you can do with publicity is to ask for a certain date range and explain the reasoning. Book retailers understand the importance and for the most part will work with you and your publisher to make certain their own customers are not frustrated with trying to make a purchase after they read, hear or see something about an author and their book.

Pre-Selling

Pre-selling your book can be an important part of any marketing campaign, as long as it's not used excessively. Teaser campaigns are a good way to build anticipation and, hopefully, demand. They alert buyers to the arrival of your title by a certain date. One way to do this is by mailing a series of postcards to book buyers or key people who can have an impact on the sale of your book. My former company used to call these people "Big Mouths," those who are more likely to catch the attention of the media, or who can be counted on to talk about a book before its publication. The hope is to create some kind of buzz. Of course, pre-selling works best when you have a track record of previous sales as a foundation for the announcement.

The pre-sale can be completed prior to the actual order from a bookseller or after the purchase as a way of reminding store personnel the title will arrive soon. Either way, you do not want to over-sell a book, providing buyers or retailers with so much material it loses its effectiveness. Pre-selling requires the right combination of teasers and information. There is a fine line between adequate pre-selling and junk mail, so it is best to pre-sell too little rather than too much.

Think Creatively

I'm sure you are tired of the phase "think outside the box," but in the case of marketing books it is essential. Publishers are concerned with keeping the production process flowing. They must continually keep books on the launch pad so they can generate billing and keep the revenue flowing. They seldom have time to sit and think creatively. Marketing becomes automatic; rarely do they come up with new ideas. They use ideas others have created that have worked in the past. This is done everyday in every marketing department in every industry that exists.

You must make the time to think creatively about marketing your book if you are self-published or with a small press. You need to give strong consideration to your audience and establish in your mind who your readers will be. Often, it helps to utilize a group of people whom you trust to be objective, creative and inventive. When marketing books, a group is better suited to thinking creatively. For whatever reason, the best book marketing lends itself to a group activity.

Use Common Sense

Here are some quick examples: if you are writing a garden book whose readers are located in a particular region of the country, why not market to nurseries or garden centers in that area? Who better to see your book than people who visit local nurseries or garden centers? You might get an opportunity to market your book in a local store for one of the big national chains. Try the local shops, the ones with ties to the community. The same logic holds true for cookbooks or any other type of non-fiction title geared to a specific audience. Work those local independent stores first and try to tie your book to the product or service they offer, this is thinking creatively.

If you are writing fiction, it is a bit harder. But let's say you are writing a medical mystery. How about a doctor's office, clinic, or medical organization that would have some connection to your book? The hope is to find a niche where you can sell your book outside the traditional marketplace where the big publishers do not venture. Tap into a group that might have an interest in what you are writing. The possibilities are endless. If one of the characters in your book has a disability, why not try to market to national organizations whose members live with the same disability? You get the picture.

Test and Then Move On

If your book—fiction or non-fiction—has ties in someway to a particular city, state or region of the country, then focus on booksellers in those areas. Don't ignore the mainstream, but also market where your audience will work, shop, seek information or travel.

Be willing to test and then move to the next idea when one does not meet your expectations. Every idea is not going to be successful. Recognize and embrace that fact. Marketing is about testing and then moving on. Set some goals, check results often and then be willing to accept the fact that an idea didn't work. It's no big deal! You've just eliminated one idea that didn't work, which gives you the opportunity to find another that will. Be different than the majors; take a moment and think about why your idea failed or succeeded and learn from that. The goal is to find ideas that do work and continue to build sales.

You've read it before and I'll say it again: the competition for readers is fierce. The more you can learn to think creatively and be willing to ask for help in selling your book, the better your chances are of being successful. There is nothing too crazy or silly. If it will generate publicity then you are to be applauded. If it sells books, you have reached one of your goals. Be adventurous and take chances. It's your hard work at stake, your future as an author. Without risk, there is little reward. You've earned the opportunity; now seize the moment.

Bringing It All Into Focus

Marketing is critical to your success as an author. Regardless of whether you are self-publishing, with a small press or a large trade publisher, the more you know about the marketplace and how to make marketing decisions, the better your chances are of maximizing your sale and minimizing your returns.

To be a good marketer you need to think creatively, coordinate your marketing efforts through to the arrival of your book in stores, be willing to go where other publishers will not and have the courage to walk up to booksellers and media outlets to promote yourself and your book. The worst that can happen is that someone will say, "No, thank you." The competition is fierce, but if you understand the goals of your competition, learn how to exploit their weakness and capitalize on their mistakes, you will greatly improve your chances at being a successful author.

Anything you can do to push your book into the public eye should be part of your marketing campaign, as long as you can make a reasonable assumption on its cost effectiveness. Good luck!

Part 4

UNDERSTANDING NUMBERS

When publishers discuss numbers, it is important to know exactly what they are talking about and which numbers are being discussed. There are four basic number possibilities publishers use when discussing books: announced first print, actual first print, total shipped and one we've already covered: budget numbers.

Announced First Print

This number has no significance to anyone other than the book buyer working for the bookseller. This number was created by publishers as a way of promoting certain titles to their customers. For example, some booksellers will not consider any title that does not suggest an announced first print of 100,000 copies. This means the buyer does not want to be presented with any book not one of the top titles in a publisher's seasonal list.

If an announced first print is 100,000, the actual first print could be as low as 25,000. There are many factors that come into play in this determination. Whenever you hear an announced first print number, remember it has no real significance to anyone other than the book buyer.

Actual First Print

The words themselves are self-explanatory; this is the actual number of an individual title the publisher first prints. Compared to an announced first print, the actual first print can be half or less, as in the previous example. The "announced" raises the level of importance for the book buyer. However, the actual total of combined purchases from all booksellers is the basis for the actual first print number. Keep in mind that sales reps sell books to their customers prior to books being printed.

It is important to keep inventory levels as low as possible so if the total orders from all booksellers on an individual title are 17,500 then the actual first print may be 18,000. The announced on this book could have been 40,000 or 50,000. Again, that number has no real significance to the author. Once the actual first print is set, the next in importance is the total shipped.

Total Shipped

This is important only as a percent of the actual first print. Publishers generally keep low inventories simply because it is relatively easy to get reprints. Even on books that are flying off the shelves, publishers are reluctant to print enough to cover the total demand. Excess inventory is costly and controls are important to maintain. If actual orders came in at 17,500 and the publisher prints 18,000, then they would ship 17,500, which is 97% of the actual first print.

Excessive inventory can result in those books being destroyed and that is not a good thing for an author's career or a publisher's bottom line. Typically, publishers will ship 95% or more of every title they print.

Budget Number

A budget number is different from all the other numbers assigned to a book. It's the actual bottom line target for the entire company. A budget number is what the sales group must ship to all booksellers combined in total number of copies—no exceptions and no excuses!

PULLING IT ALL TOGETHER

Let's summarize everything up to this point: the sales and marketing department sets budgets each fall for the following calendar year. Each sales manager and national account person is given the list of titles on a spreadsheet by month and position on the list. Books are given a budget number based on a variety of factors.

In an ideal publishing world, the budget number would have some basis for its assignment to a title, usually sales history of the author or category. There are plenty of sales reports that can provide numbers to predict what any given title might sell net at retail. However, in today's publishing world, that realism is thrown out the window and the budget is based on the company's overall need to generate total gross billing, not what the list can reasonably expect to sell at retail.

The Budget is Set

With the new budget numbers, the sales and marketing group breaks the overall budget up by title and assigns the goals to sales representatives (for their individual territory) and to the national accounts, hopefully spreading the pain across the board to as many as possible. Now, based on the new aggressive budgets, each book is given an announced first print number.

For book buyers, technology means they can easily access any author's sales history. The one thing a book buyer does not pay close attention to when looking at sales history is the gross amount they bought. They look at the net sale of a book to make the determination of whether or not they will buy the next title or in what quantity. There is no flag in their computer that indicates an over-sold or over-distributed situation, so if the sell-through is less than 60% (and especially if it's less than 50%), then the chances of getting your next book bought at the same level of the last is slim and can result in a zero order.

Overcoming Objections

Sell-through is one criterion a book buyer uses when deciding whether or not to purchase a particular book. One of the most difficult facts to explain to a buyer is why a book had a poor sales performance. When an author's first book fails to meet expectations, even for good reasons, selling a second book, or even a third, is tough to do. Failure for any author's subsequent books after that first poor sell-through is not only tough, but almost impossible to overcome, especially if the same house is publishing the author.

In an attempt to overcome the objections of a poor sell-through when selling a new title, publishers will throw around numbers and terms to try and baffle those who lack a basic understanding of the business. Obviously this does not work with book buyers or industry insiders, but it is often used on agents and authors who question the net sale and sell-through of their books.

If an author has a poor track record or sales history and the company must get higher numbers on subsequent books for budgetary reasons, they will set a high announced first print on that title. The book buyer, recognizing the way in which the publisher tries to gloss over past sales will often refuse higher orders, but may settle for numbers that do not drop the title completely out of contention for minimal distribution. This is one way sales departments use numbers to overcome objections.

Basic Facts

Let's examine some facts: It is conservatively estimated there are at least five hundred titles published every single day by major trade publishers. That is over one hundred and eighty thousand titles in a calendar year. Many question whether this number includes all of the medium-sized houses and the small presses, self-published or print-on-demand companies.

Currently, there are over five thousand retail bookstores (including the big chain stores, regional chain stores and the independently owned retail bookstores). In addition, there are easily another five thousand major retail outlets where books are sold, and this is only recognizing the major ones. While there are actually more than ten thousand retail outlets, for the sake of this discussion let's stick with that number.

With over one hundred and eighty thousand total titles and ten thousand major retail outlets, you get a picture of why the competition is so fierce. The marketplace is only so big; it can only absorb so many titles in certain quantities. When the marketplace is glutted with books, oversold and over-distributed, it can't maintain its own natural balance. Publishers are responsible for the problem, because the unreasonable expectations they place on titles typically far exceed the natural distribution level for their books.

What does all this mean? It means the publishing industry is in a quandary and the pressure to meet corporate financial goals far outweighs the needs of books and their authors. Inflated budgets trigger a vicious cycle. It goes on each and every year and the pressure to surpass the previous year, regardless of the strength of the books on the list, grows in intensity.

While the sales department is laboring over preparing budgets, the daily grind does not stop. Sales data on current titles has to be collected from customers. Updates on each current title have to be prepared for executive management. Planning for the upcoming lists has to continue and through all of this the department must continue to hit the numbers, show growth and always feed that monster.

It's worth mentioning the 90/10 rule again. If you are an author who falls into that 90% range and your book is part of the list generating less than 10% of the company's gross billing, you absolutely must know what all of this means and what you can do about it. You start by understanding the total market for selling books, how budgets are set and the relationship between the sale and distribution of your book.

The Book in this Example

(1) There was an **announced first print** of 50,000, which we know has no relationship to the budget or any other number. It is merely a marketing tool the sales group used to get the attention of big customers or booksellers. An impressive number here dramatically increases the possibility of this book getting larger initial orders, which helps to achieve the overall gross dollar-billing amount.

(2) The **actual budget number**, the total number of copies the company needs to distribute is 20,000. That number has no relationship to the announced first print number or what the sales group feels has a realistic chance of selling net at retail. This number is what the publisher must ship in total copies to the marketplace to generate their overall revenue target.

(3) The **realistic budget** is that number the sales executives assigned to the book during the first round of the budget process based on sales history and thorough research is 10,000, which has no relationship to the actual budget, announced first print or any other number.

(4) The **actual first print** is 18,000, which is close to the actual budget of 20,000 and is the number the company is actually having printed.

(5) The company **is shipping** 17,500, which means that out of the 18,000 only 500 copies will remain in the warehouse. The rest of the 17,500 will be shipped to customers.

After you understand what all of the above numbers mean, the next important point to remember is the distribution. Certainly these numbers and their meanings are important, but above all else you need to know where the 17,500 copies are going, to which customers and in what quantity. This is important to manage the proper sell-through. To understand distribution you must know what the numbers mean and how they impact distribution.

What to Do?

So who has the power to stop this debacle? Corporate ownership and their top executives certainly bear the brunt of the burden because they refuse to accept the truth about today's book publishing marketplace. It is an extremely mature market where the total number of book buying consumers is not growing. People do not read nor buy books as much as they used to.

Publishers have a huge share of the responsibility for the prices they are willing to pay top authors. This is the same as with any field of entertainment, including professional sports. Some authors are being paid far in excess of what publishers can reasonably expect in return and this hurts all of the writers who want to be authors. But who can blame those highly paid authors? This process will not change until the writers and authors learn how to take some control over their books. They begin to take control by understanding the basics of the business of publishing.

MARKET SHARE

When authors sit down with publishers to discuss the sales of their book(s) the sales group is confident they can provide enough confusing information to explain anything and make it look as though the company is doing everything they can to support an individual title. One of the ways they do this is to start a discussion about market shares. Don't be fooled; here is all you need to know in order to cut through the smoke and mirrors:

Market share is one of the ways a publisher measures the amount of business their booksellers represent when compared to the total number of books sold. You don't need to be an expert in the calculation of a publisher's market share to understand the basis for how it is used. You need to know what the language means and how it is used by your publisher.

Every bookseller has a market share. How your publisher makes that calculation should be the starting point of any discussion. There are two basic methods for calculating a bookseller's market share: gross, which is based on the total number of copies shipped; and net, which is based on the total net copies sold. If a salesperson whips out a big sheet of paper and starts to explain your sales based on market shares, the two questions you should ask are, how were the market shares calculated and how often are the market shares calculated?

Gross Market Share

This calculation is based on the number of total copies shipped of an individual title or group of titles. For example, let's say a publisher has shipped a total of one hundred thousand copies of a single title. Gross market share is calculated based upon how the one hundred thousand copies are broken down into actual orders and distributed to customers.

The first number in this example (gross) represents the actual order and the second number (percent of gross) represents the percentage of the one hundred thousand copies shipped. This percentage would represent each bookseller's gross market share.

Bookseller Type	Gross	% of Gross
Chain Bookstores	25,000	25%
Membership Clubs	25,000	25%
Mass Merchants	20,000	20%
Book Jobbers	10,000	10%
Ind. Distributors	5,000	5%
Ind. Bookstores	5,000	5%
Internet Booksellers	5,000	5%
Specialty Retailers	5,000	5%
	100,000	100%

Net Market Share

This calculation is based on the number of net copies of an individual title sold. For example, let's say a publisher has shipped a total of one hundred thousand copies of a single title and the net sale after many months of returns is fifty-five thousand. How that net number is disbursed is the basis for how net market share is calculated.

Again, take the major customer types below. The first number in this example (net) represents the total net sale for each customer. The next set of numbers (percent of net) represents the net market share of each customer type and is based on their total net sale of the Individual title.

Bookseller Type	Net	% of Net
Chain Bookstores	15,000	27%
Membership Clubs	12,000	22%
Mass Merchants	8,000	15%
Book Jobbers	6,000	11%
Ind. Distributors	2,000	4%
Ind. Bookstores	4,000	7%
Internet Booksellers	4,000	7%
Specialty Retailers	4,000	7%
	55,000	100%

Again, this is an oversimplified example of net market share where the total shipped was one hundred thousand copies with a total net of fifty-five thousand copies.

Do Not Be Confused

Sell-through has nothing to do with market share. Don't let anyone in-house try to confuse you with the language. Both examples of gross and net market share are not to be confused with sell-through, also referred to as percent of sale. Take the retail chain bookstores used in the previous two examples: their gross market share was 25%, the net market share was 27% and their sell-through on this single title would be 60%.

For example, 15,000 net copies sold ÷ 25,000 total shipped copies = 60%.

Now you have a brief explanation of market shares and the calculation of sell-through or percent of sale.

The Final Question

Now that you have an understanding of gross and net market share, there is one final question to the market share discussion that must be addressed. How often do publishers calculate market shares? Publishers who do not recalculate market shares seasonally—at least three times a year—are working from old data that throws the numbers completely out of whack.

The business of publishing and bookselling is constantly changing. There are shifts in the overall distribution of titles on a seasonal basis. Retailers can change distributors, build new stores, close old stores, and so on. The result of this constant shift in the dynamic marketplace means book buyers are continually looking at sales and making determinations on how best to adjust their buys to improve sell-through and increase the number of total units sold.

As a result of these changes, market shares must be recalculated on a seasonal basis, both by account type and category mix, both gross and net. It is not uncommon for publishers to go years without readjusting market shares and this makes for poor planning, inefficient sales reporting and bad numbers across the board.

When you get to the point where you are having discussions with your publisher about the sales and distribution of your book and the subject of market shares comes up, remember to ask those two all important questions: how were the market shares calculated and how often were they calculated? Both questions will alert the sales group that you know what you are talking about.

WHERE THE RUBBER MEETS THE ROAD

Now we get to where it all starts to come together. This is the point where the work of the sales and marketing group begins to take shape. This is typically an area overlooked by authors and underestimated by editors and agents. Proper distribution is the key to a high sell-through and is what you need to be a successful author. To understand distribution you need to be clear on everything we have covered to this point.

Over-weighted

When publishers ask "What is the distribution?" they want to know how many copies are being shipped to which customer. Each bookseller knows their capability, which means they know exactly how many copies they can buy and place to maximize the sale. Whether it is in-store or to a reseller such as a jobber or distributor, book customers know how many copies are needed for merchandising and how many are to be held back as inventory.

As an example, independent bookstores around the country have a good idea how many copies of a particular category book they can sell. Based on years of retail experience, they have a good idea how many Sandra Brown copies they will sell, as well as Nora Roberts, Tom Clancy, and the like. They also know how many mid-list fiction, non-fiction, business, romance, western and science fiction category books they can sell. If they underestimate that number they can always place reorders for copies through the publisher, distributor or jobber. If they overestimate, they can return the product.

As a total number, let's say a typical independent bookstore sells thirty copies in the mystery category, in a month. Based on their current inventory they will typically only buy thirty copies. The seasonal list of titles from each publisher is evaluated and purchases are made on an assortment of thirty total copies: three copies of ten individual mystery titles. Customers know what they can sell. Sales history is used to determine the quantity of copies needed to fill the anticipated demand for the product. Now this is a simple example, because there are many factors that go into how many copies of each title are purchased at any given time, but for the sake of this discussion, let's continue to keep it simple.

If a bookseller knows they can sell thirty copies in a particular category and yet they purchase forty copies, then they are over-weighted and the net result will typically be a heavier than normal return of the books. Take this one step up the ladder and the same holds true for publishers. If they are selling a category book they know by customer type how many each can sell. Yet when the final orders come in they discover they are shipping entirely too many copies to a particular customer type. What happens? Nothing! Publishing houses never turn down billing, so the unsuspecting author who put their faith and trust in their publisher to purchase, print and distribute their category book now has reduced her chance of having a good sell-through simply because she was not aware of what was happening.

Sales History

When you can go down the list of every customer type, each bookseller will know how many copies of which author, category or format of book they can sell. This is why the sales history of an author is important. These customers keep detailed sales records, usually dating back three years, on the performance of authors. A bad history is extremely difficult to overcome. The bigger the customer, the larger the total numbers ordered and so the more detailed the sales history they can track.

Booksellers know how many copies they can sell net, yet continue to order larger and larger quantities. Keep in mind, when a publisher is paying a fee or allowance for buying a certain quantity of a title, the bookseller can receive payment and still return the book for full credit. Of course, it doesn't make sense for the bigger booksellers to warehouse books, even temporarily, but it is part of doing business in the world of publishing.

With the goal of shipping as many copies to as many booksellers as possible, publishers do not take the time to evaluate the correct quantity of which book should go to which account. Certainly they run their own sales history that should closely duplicate that of the customer, but they make buy recommendations based on the need to sell more and more copies. Every time a sales representative goes into a book buyer's office to sell a seasonal list of titles, they know how many copies that bookseller has sold of every key title and they also know how many they need to convince the buyer to take in order to meet their budget requirements.

Publishers figure, the bigger the book customer, the greater the potential for a large buy. This typically corresponds with a higher recommended number. Trying to squeeze copies out of small customers doesn't make sense. The sales reps are dealing with too many accounts and it is substantially more difficulty to make any discernable increase in a gross number. However, when the buy runs into several thousand copies, then the better the opportunity to dramatically increase the initial buys through only a handful of customers.

Distribution Based on Budgets

Distribution is based on the budget numbers developed for each title. A higher budget creates the requisite need for a larger and wider distribution. There are obvious factors on the sale of each title that have to make sense. For example, the rep would not attempt to sell a literary title to a supermarket or drug store. Not only would the book buyer recognize the mistake, that purchase would damage the credibility of the salesperson. In turn, the latest trashy novel might not belong in an urban bookstore that caters to world travelers. These are the obvious examples; the not so blatant examples are where the net sale on a book gets hurt.

The publisher entices the bookseller to buy many more copies than are predictable in hopes of increasing the number shipped. Of course, there is hope the copies will sell well, but the real reason would be to meet the billing demands of the parent corporation. This is the kind of over-distribution where authors are totally uninformed about the consequences. The only way to stop these kinds of situations from occurring is to create relationships in-house and be involved in the development of the numbers in the course of bringing your book to publication.

Every publisher knows how many copies can reasonably be sold into the independent bookstores across the country, the book jobbers, the independent distributors, mass merchants, chain bookstores and so on. They also know the percent of total gross and net copies that each bookseller represents. When a person evaluates the buy across the board of all booksellers and knows, for example, that mass merchants represent fifteen percent of the distribution of a mid-list hardcover romance, then someone should question the veracity of a distribution where they represent twenty-five percent. However, in the world of publishing, that sales group would be applauded.

If you are an author and your editor calls to tell you the initial distribution on your book was twenty thousand and the original budget was for twenty thousand, the first thing you would want to know is where those copies are going. If, for example, only five thousand units were being shipped to bookstores and the remaining fifteen thousand were going to jobbers or distributors, you should be concerned. Copies being shipped to a jobber or a distributor are being warehoused until they receive reorders from retailers. The ratio of 3-to-1 is not considered a good distribution. A sale to a distributor means the publisher is hoping for retail success so those distributors can then resell their inventory of your book as reorders to the bookstores.

If you are wondering how you would ever get this kind of information about your book – you ask.

Summary of Distribution

In a perfect world, books belong with the right book customer in the correct quantity, no exceptions. Publishers sell too many titles in any given season to spend time considering the fate of each and every one. The more you know about the market, booksellers and numbers, the better chance you have of making a positive impact, which results in a higher sell-through on the publication of your book. Distribution should make sense and, depending on the genre of your book, you should know which bookseller has the greatest potential to maximize the chances of your book being successful. This translates into selling more net copies at retail than are returned. This will go a long way toward guaranteeing your future as an author.

Getting distribution information from a publisher is not an easy task because publishers resist sharing too much information with writers. However, if you follow these guidelines and learn to ask the right questions, you can improve your chances of becoming a successfully published author.

OPPORTUNITIES FOR WRITERS

On occasion, publishers will launch a new series of books within an existing category. From a sales and marketing standpoint, when a publisher packages two, three or four books together and gives those a similar cover look, they're referred to as a series. This is an ideal way to increase distribution, market share within a category and hopefully net sales. Typically, a new series is launched in mass market paperback because publishers can do so much with relatively little cost and have a much wider distribution network that gives them a lot more bang for their marketing buck.

Books Sell in Cycles

Category publishing tends to sell in cycles; sometimes the cycle can be hastened along by something that happens in the entertainment field, such as a new movie with tons of publicity or a change in the new season lineup for television. One example was when the NBC series *Law & Order* was first released and it became obvious the show would be a hit. Editors quickly went looking for cop books, police procedurals or anything that would closely resemble a *Law & Order* story line.

Soon after this shift in the marketplace, readers began to see more titles based around forensic police work. Then the central characters in more thriller novels became cops or criminal investigators. This so-called cycle quickly jumped the track and became its own genre or category and will remain strong as long as today's major best-selling authors continue to write novels where the police or private investigators are the central characters. Certainly the authors will write them as long as the public continues to buy their books.

Category sales cycles can turn quickly and there has to be sufficient evidence the trend will continue to increase or the series idea will be dropped. Major category sales trends in romance, mystery, science fiction, even non-fiction, move slowly. However, those sub-categories or genres can change overnight. This is the reason publishers like to create a series that can straddle the fence, with not too much of a sub-category while still maintaining a touch of the mainstream.

Editors knowledgeable about the competition in their category of expertise will notice an increase in the number of single titles that fall into a sub-genre, outside the mainstream category. When this happens they will closely monitor the package, price and net sales. If they sense a change in the direction of the mainstream category and the number of single titles being published into this sub-genre, they will begin to look for manuscripts to fill the niche. This is an opportunity for writers. Editors can become especially aggressive if they do not have titles on the publication schedule and they see the competition is beating them to the street.

Now that the editor has found a sufficient number of sub-genre titles to publish, they spread the books over a period of months and wait to see if the sales remain constant. They follow the trend of the category to watch for increases in copies sold that reflect a consumer interest in the new sub-category. If there is a distinct spike in sales over a period of months, discussions will begin on how to increase distribution and capture sales on this new sub-genre cycle. This will lead to a new series and possibly into an entirely new imprint.

Launch of a New Series

The unfortunate part about the launch of a new series is that, beyond the spike in a handful of category titles over a few months, there is absolutely no research done on the breadth or depth of the sub-genre. Publishing is done on instinct and, more times than not, the new series will slowly wither away and fall into oblivion from lack of sales to the consumer. Publishers realize that to be on the cutting edge of the marketplace and gain a jump on the competition they need to try new books in new sub-categories. Their investment is small compared to the investment in time and effort made by the authors of these books.

When the decision is made to launch the new series, the editor has to be certain they have plenty of these new sub-genre books under contract. The success or failure of the launch can often depend on the publisher's ability to supply the market. Seldom does an editor have problems finding new books. They may even go so far as to ask struggling writers under contract to change the focus of their new manuscript to fit the new series. This could be an opportunity for writers to reposition themselves. But, if the series fails, so might the future of the struggling writer.

Since the new series will be launched as mass market paperbacks, the numbers are different than your typical hardcover. The distribution for mass market books extends far beyond that of a new hardcover. Included are supermarkets, drug stores, military bases, airport terminals, mass merchants and so on. The only hardcover books that can and do get distribution into these types of accounts are best-selling authors, but the numbers are much smaller than the mass market titles. Also, mid-list hardcover titles are virtually excluded from these outlets unless there is a direct tie-in to the region of the country.

Non-best-selling mass market paperbacks, described as category titles, will sell initially in numbers fewer than fifty thousand copies. Most will fall into the twenty-to-thirty thousand-copy range or below. This indicates the emphasis on bestsellers in this marketplace. Mass market bestsellers are purchased months in advance of publication and the numbers range for titles positioned at number twenty on the list to the number one book for the month. Titles on the lower end of the bestseller card may see initial numbers in the fifty thousand-copy range all the way to eight hundred thousand and above. The goals for most publishers when launching a new series in mass market paperback is around one hundred thousand copies out the door on the first month of the launch and that will include all titles included in the launch.

The biggest books are always positioned at the top of the list and are the ones the publisher expects to be placed on the upcoming bestseller list. When you get to the third title on the list (and, for some publishers, the second on the list), the orders they get from book buyers can drop substantially. With the launch of a new series, the publisher hopes the entire package of titles will get a distribution far in excess of what the same number of titles would get if sold individually. This is why the launch of a series needs bigger numbers collectively to help increase the market share of a particular category.

The marketplace is shrinking. This problem spans the entire range of the publishing industry. There are fewer placement opportunities for books regardless of their format or trim size. The launch of a new series means more copies will flood the booksellers, which means the shelf life of existing titles will drop and returns will increase.

Mass market book buyers buy only enough titles to fill the space they have and to fill a particular distribution. They know how many titles they need each month to fill the pockets in a particular category. When publishers launch a new series, the number of titles being offered by all publishers will far exceed what the book buyer needs to fill the space. The only way most book buyers will take a chance on these new titles is if the publisher offers a sweet enough incentive.

Ready to Launch

The publisher now has a series of new titles set to launch, all with a new cover design, lower price point and the need to come up with a hefty incentive. Most will launch with a lower price point than the category is used to seeing in an attempt to attract the consumer to the new look. In addition to the lower price point, the book buyer will be offered additional discount points or promotional/advertising dollars for ordering a large enough number on all of the books in the launch.

Competitive publishers will follow suit, either at the same time or quickly thereafter. The result is a flood of new books into the marketplace within a short period of time which, of course, causes book buyers to purchase more copies than they need. This eventually results in a larger than normal return. If this new series represents your chance to get your first book published, you have a difficult decision to make. There are few perfect opportunities to become a first time author, so you have to learn to make the best of what you have to work with. The first thing you want to do is understand the series, the category and the goals of the publisher. You can learn this by asking the right questions:

1.   ***What are the marketing plans for the new launch?***
     Your publisher should have plenty of information

regarding exactly how the company plans to promote the new series. There should be an entire lineup of advertisements aimed directly at the target audience. They should be loaded with merchandising ideas such as floor and counter displays. They should be able to show you a timeline on exactly when the advertising and promotion starts prior, during and after the launch.

2. ***How much advertising, promotion and marketing dollars has the company committed to the launch?***

Rather than allow someone to give you a number, ask for details on how the money will be spent. You are looking for some indication that the dollars are committed and the spending is well thought out. You are not looking for specifics, but you want a general idea that the plans are in place and the money is dedicated to certain areas.

3. ***What is the expected distribution on each of the titles?***

Realizing there are several titles packaged together as part of the initial launch, you want some idea on what the goals will be for each book. Goals would represent the actual numbers the company hopes to distribute at launch. Have some awareness if the numbers are far in excess of what was previously discussed. Be surprised if they fall below the levels mentioned earlier. Balance is the key to getting the right number of copies shipped initially. To be successful, you must distribute the right number of total copies.

4. ***Are incentives being offered to book buyers to meet the sales goals of the company?***

A simple yes will not be enough. You need details on what kinds of incentives are being offered. Certainly, at this point you might be telling yourself that your publisher is not going to share all of this information with a first-time author. You are probably correct. However, by asking these questions, you are sending a very strong signal that you are aware of the marketplace and you are concerned with your future as an author.

5. ***Does the incentive include a lower retail price?***
Again, you need more than a simple yes. The company should be able to tell you the plans regarding the lower retail price. This is where your knowledge in your particular category pays off. You should know whether that price is close to the average or well below the other books published in your category. A retail price that is too low is not a good idea, because it will give the publisher artificial sales that can never be duplicated when the titles revert to a normal retail price, which might cause consumers to walk away at the end of the launch. This will not help your career as an author.

6. ***How long will the incentives be in place?***
This is a very important question because the answers will give you a good idea of the publisher's commitment to the program. If there were no current plans to lower the price or take away the discounts then it would appear they are fully committed. Typically, six months after the launch, the price and discounts go away. Sometimes it is a gradual change over the course of a year or more. The longer the timeframe the more the company is willing to put their neck on the line to make this launch pay off.

7. *What is the acceptable return percentage for the launch?*

Return percentage is the other side of sell-through and represents the percentage of books returned versus sold. A 60% sell-through of a title would result in a 40% return percentage.

This can be difficult for any publisher to answer. Perhaps they haven't given the question any serious thought. Any publisher that goes through the process of launching a new series or imprint will know exactly when they can pull the incentives and raise the retail price based on the number of copies they ship and how many come back. Often times they will not decide to pull the plug until after they can more accurately predict in which direction the launch will go.

Confirm the Commitment

All of these questions and the assortment of answers should give you one clear signal: whether or not your publisher is willing to commit the resources needed to make this launch a success. All you need is a positive indication that your book, as part of the launch, will get a good opportunity to experience a high sell-through at retail. Please be aware: it's more than likely you will not get answers to all of these questions, but asking is important. In order to alert your publisher you understand the basics of the business and that you know that your career depends on a good sell-through percentage, you must at least ask.

Sometimes the answers are not as important as the questions because what those people tell you may give you a good idea about whether or not this is a publisher you want handling your book. You are only a first-time author once and you want to get it right, even if you have to turn down what you think is a golden opportunity. I am not suggesting you turn down the opportunity, but you want to get off on the right foot. Your awareness of the market should tell everyone in-house you are knowledgeable and your book deserves attention.

If you decide to take the opportunity, find a way to have a discussion with someone in the sales department. During the launch of this new series, if there are a number of books bundled together each month, some titles may have lower sales expectations than others. For example, if a publisher launches four titles in the first few months, they may drop to three or even two titles a month from that point forward. If this is the case, then the top two titles during the initial phase will probably have higher budget numbers assigned to them than the other two.

It would benefit you to discuss with someone in sales, preferably someone in a management position, which position they think would be best for your book. More than likely, you will have absolutely no impact on the position of your book. This will have been decided based upon how much money you received in your contract, but it would still benefit you to ask the question. All of these questions are strong signals to the key people that you are on top of the situation and your goal is a high sell-through.

Of course, the answers are important but the questions are key. Awareness in-house of an author who understands what is going on can make all the difference in the world.

Your career as a writer hinges upon your book's ability to sell more copies than are returned. Failure could spell doom for your future as an author. If you want to write full time and earn a nice living doing so, spend some time learning the business and understanding the basics. Being part of the launch of a new series or imprint could be a big break for you as an author. Know the questions to ask, learn how to evaluate the information you get back and continue to send the signal that you know something about the business side of publishing.

WHEN YOUR BOOK GETS SPECIAL ATTENTION

One day your phone rings and your editor is excited to tell you that your upcoming book has been selected as a "focus" title on the next seasonal list. You are thrilled, overcome with emotion, you fumble for words, cannot think of questions to ask, so you thank the editor for her support and express appreciation for your publisher's efforts. The glow that surrounds you is apparent to everyone you come into contact with over the next few days, maybe weeks.

For the purposes of this chapter, keep in mind the word "focus" could be synonymous with any word a publisher might use to designate a title separated from the rest on a seasonal list. This separation might be nothing more than a designation to a small number of titles or by a special marketing program where few titles are part of a group. By selecting a focus title (or small group) your publisher is sending the signal to everyone in-house that they must keep their eye on those special titles.

What This Means

The fact that any title is selected as a "focus" on a seasonal list can mean only one thing. Start with the premise that publishers always need billing. The need to generate revenue to meet budgets to exceed projections is the foundation of what major trade publishers face in today's competitive environment. The selection of a "focus" title is used as a marketing tool to segregate the list and bring focus to a particular title or group of titles.

Let's establish some facts as a way of helping explain this particular situation: the author received little in the form of an advance for his or her manuscript and the special attention is totally and completely unexpected. Since the contract was signed with the publisher there has been little or no contact with the editor up to the phone call announcing the "focus" designation. This sudden special attention can be used to your advantage if you lay the groundwork for your success in-house.

The Potential in the Marketplace

Once the publishing schedule is set and the budget process completed, the sales group will often closely scrutinize each title for its potential in the marketplace. The budget numbers for the seasonal list will be set in concrete and will never be reduced, so the group is always looking for books that can be brought up to the next level, titles they can "run with." Since the books that anchor each publication list have the highest budgets, secondary or mid-list titles are the ones that receive closer examination. The sales group is looking for those books whose budgets can be raised significantly as a way to help fill the anticipated shortfall.

When your book is selected as a "focus" title, the sales and marketing group has decided your book is one that could possibly fill a gap in the budget process and help to overcome the deficit that descends every publishing season. This means salespeople have read your manuscript, liked the story and feel your book can help to fill the numbers void.

They are looking for those gems in the seasonal list that can be turned into something special by giving it a "focus" designation and getting higher than anticipated initial orders and a much larger distribution than normal.

To elevate a title on the list, approval has to be sought from the editor (who, in my experience, has never refused) and of course the publisher. If the sales department feels strongly enough about a particular title or group of titles to make them a "focus" then typically approval is unanimous. Now, decisions have to be made on the budgets and how much to raise the numbers.

At the editorial or acquisitions meeting (as an example)' where your book was first bought, the profit and loss statement indicated the company needed to sell ten thousand copies at a $25.00 retail price with a sell-through of sixty percent to break even. These numbers mean the title would be perfect for the "focus" designation. The company has little investment and fairly low expectations, if the title sells better than expected as a "focus," it is a homerun. If it doesn't, there will always be another group of books next season.

Going From 30 to 100

When the "focus" designation is assigned to your book, what would have been an announced first print of say thirty thousand will jump to the more aggressive one hundred thousand, reflecting its new status on the list. Your book is starting to receive attention from book buyers. The sales group has given it an extra push and the final numbers start to pour in. You discover your book has gone from an actual first print of twenty thousand to sixty thousand.

With an announced of one hundred thousand and a first print of sixty thousand, the actual numbers out the door should be around fifty-eight thousand, with the remaining two thousand copies held back as inventory. So the sales group had taken what should have been an actual first print of twenty thousand and increased it by three hundred percent. As an author, you will be ecstatic and your editor and agent are most likely over the moon. However, this scenario creates lots of questions and you need to be able to ask them to make the most of your situation.

First and foremost, you must understand your book was selected for its potential to sell in the marketplace, which is a good thing. Several people had to have read the early manuscript and loved your writing and story. Secondly, the package had to be just right, meaning everyone loved the look, or the cover, or the price and felt that along with your writing this book had the potential to be taken to the next level. Third and finally, the company had little investment in you and your book, which makes it a prime candidate for the "focus" designation. Your book, and especially your contract, had the highest potential to fill that budget shortfall because the financial risk of failure by pushing copies out the door was less than other books on the seasonal list.

Each season, the company typically selects "focus" titles. The sales and marketing group wants booksellers to feel like these designated titles are in fact "special," but as far as the publisher is concerned, you need to keep in mind that the program is more important than the books themselves.

Segmenting the List

The "focus" program resumes each season. The reason for the program is to gain market share and generate additional revenue. This is how the sales department attempts to increase revenue by breaking the seasonal list of titles into segments and separating those "special" books into existing programs making "focus" titles more than merely books on a list. During my twenty-plus years of experience, I have seen this play out many times and the success to failure ratio, depending on your definition of success, is varied. If you are an author and your editor comes to you with a proposal that is supposed to knock your socks off, be aware! Know what questions to ask.

Here are twelve tasks to complete and questions to ask to take full advantage of this particular situation.

1. *Meet the person in charge of sales and marketing.*

   Ask you editor for an introduction. Special attention must be placed on this person. He or she will more than likely be in charge of both sales and marketing, but if not, you want the name of the boss and the head of either sales or marketing. From this point forward, these people are key to your book becoming successful. You want to have a conversation with both people.

2. *Find the name of your local sales representative.*

   This would be your publisher's representative located either in your area of the country or who travels to your part of the country to sell books. You can obtain this information from the head of sales. Sometimes they will be reluctant and, if so, your correspondence will have to go through the corporate office. You want everyone to know you are willing and able to do whatever you can in your area of the country to help in the sale of your book. This communication is much more personal than #4.

3. *Find the names and positions (titles) of the people in-house who worked on your book.*

Call your editor and get the names as quickly as possible. Start with the advertising, publicity and art departments. You want the names of those who had a direct hand in working on your book as well as the names of the department heads. This is a key factor in getting your book published successfully.

4. ***Find the names and addresses of every sales and national account person who sold your book.***
Tell the head of sales and marketing you want to show your appreciation and to offer your assistance. More than likely they will ask you to send your correspondence to the corporate office and let them distribute it to the salespeople. This is typical; publishers want to prevent authors from obtaining the home addresses and phone numbers of the salespeople. They are worried this privilege will be abused. Go along and send each a thank you card and small gift through the corporate office.

5. ***Find the name(s) of the people responsible for your book being selected as a "focus" title.***
It could be anyone from any department, but most likely the folks responsible will be from the sales and marketing area. There are probably several people who read your book and loved it enough to push for the "focus" designation. Your editor can help you find out who were the catalysts for this selection.

6. ***Find the name of the key personnel at your local bookstores.***
The success of your book may depend largely on how well it performs in your part of the country and especially in your own backyard. Familiarity with the key people at the local and regional bookstores is important for in-store appearances that should boost

your sales. Try to get to know these people before your book goes on sale. If you do not know these people, then approaching them after your book is on the market may result in him or her seeing you as someone looking for special treatment. Be careful, you do not want to alienate these folks.

7. *Put some effort into either creating or finding a very special set of cards to be sent to everyone in the company who played a part in your book's success.*

Start with the CEO, President, publisher and of course, your editor. Include a small gift, nothing extravagant, just meaningful and personal. Your note to these people is something you should expect them to read in meetings to everyone in the company. It is a way of saying thank you to everyone, professionally. It is also a way of separating yourself from all the other authors by showing your appreciation.

Never duplicate cards and gifts, if one name is on one list and then appears on another, make sure you send only one gift and one card per person. Otherwise, it appears too automatic and staged as opposed to appreciative and personal. The card and gift should be different and meaningful to each of the six groups listed previously. You are showing appreciation for their belief in your book and you are separating your book from all the other titles on the seasonal list. This is an important statement to make to the employees of your publishing house. Do not take it lightly.

8. *Ask the head of marketing to send you copies of all the materials being produced to market your book.*

Ask for brochures, sell sheets, catalog pages, anything

and everything that mentions your book as part of the "focus" title program. Say you want to share this material with your readers and friends around the country. Do not rely on your editor for this information. It is important you go through the sales and marketing departments. You need to start building a relationship with these people and you do this by being appreciative and offering your help in anyway.

9. ***Ask how your book is being advertised.***
If you cannot find this information in the material you receive or you want more detailed information, you must ask. The majority of the allocated dollars will probably be spent on ads directly to booksellers instead of to the print media. Perhaps there will be some marketing spent on print advertisements in your local or regional area of the country. If not, you should make this suggestion. Of course, it will depend on how much money is left in the budget. The success of your book may very well start in your area of the country.

10. ***Ask how your book is being promoted.***
Your publisher should be making every effort to get you interviews with the newspapers in your region and key publications around the country. In addition, he should secure appearances on local and regional television stations as well as bookstores in your geographic area. Never volunteer as an author to do things your publisher should do for you. If you see the marketing plans and something is missing, ask them to fill the void for you.

11. ***Ask where those 58,000 copies are being shipped.***
This question comes very late in the process after the book has been sold and purchase orders are received

for your book. The answer will dictate your response. For example, if a very large percentage of the copies are being shipped to one bookseller then you should ask the head of sales if there is any way you can have contact with that bookseller via in-store appearances, a luncheon to meet the book buyer or anything to place your face with your book. These booksellers need to marry your face and charming personality with your book as a way of separating it from all the rest.

12. *Ask how the 58,000 copies are going to be spread among the booksellers.*

This will give you a sense of which booksellers are key to your book's success and will give you a small chance of making yourself known to them. This is typically done in advance of your book being sold, however, the effort is worth a try. Your goal here is to make connections with as many book buyers as possible as a way of saying thank you for their support. In addition, ask if there is anything you can do in-store to help them sell books.

Success Means Selling Copies

As I have described to the audience at my seminars and workshops, getting your book successfully published means selling as many copies at retail as possible. This is absolutely the most important thing that can happen to you as an author. Selling more does not mean getting large quantities of your book distributed, it means getting them sold. Just because your book has received special attention by being selected as a "focus" title that does not mean it will be successful.

If you were the author in this example and you did not get the answers to all of the above questions, then you were way behind schedule in getting the attention in-house that you needed. Even if you have not taken all the proper steps before your book gets published, you can still use the added attention of being an author of a "focus" title to correct some earlier mistakes.

Once your book is sold and the orders are collected, the distribution is complete. This means you have absolutely no chance of trying to convince the sales group your book deserves a better or different distribution. In the situation described here, the distribution is complete and all you are trying to do after the fact is say thank you and offer your assistance.

Your book has been sold to as wide a group of booksellers as possible with as many copies as possible. The goal of the sales group in this situation was to increase the numbers for the budget; your title was used for that purpose. All you have to do now is hope you get a good sell-through. The ultimate problem with special attention created to fill a budget gap is that the quantities of your book going to certain booksellers may not present the best chance at selling a lot of copies, which is what you need to be successful with your subsequent books.

Summarizing My Points

Let's summarize: you have a book being given special attention. Your book has been sold and distributed; the orders far exceed what you expect. Now you are racing to get answers to key questions and make the most of this attention by establishing the right kind of contact with key personnel within the company. Even though your efforts may go largely unnoticed and you may not have time to make the most of this "focus" designation, you need to make your best effort and be realistic. Sometimes a kind word, a thank you and a personal gift can make all the difference. Even if your book has not been sold and distributed properly, a sales rep all the way across the country can influence returns to a certain extent. Your gesture of appreciation can go a long way towards the sales rep asking a book buyer or bookseller to redistribute copies rather than return them.

A quick word about gifts: one time, a famous best-selling author wanted to show appreciation to the sales force for a successful launch of a new book. This author spent a lot of money buying each sales representative around the country an expensive bottle of champagne. Not that the gesture wasn't appreciated, but the author could have made a much better impression on the group if a gift card to dinner at a national chain restaurant had been sent. An expensive bottle of champagne does not make the same impression as something they can use for their family. The author would have spent far less money and the gift would have been appreciated more. Keep in mind that for sales representatives and national account people, this is a job, it just happens to be selling books.

Crashing the List

Everything discussed in the last segment regarding focus titles is exactly the same when a book crashes the list. The only difference is that everything is accelerated and placed on a much faster track. To review, crashing the list means your publisher desperately needs billing and they want to take advantage of a situation in the market, so they take a title under contract, or search for one that fits the hole in their seasonal publication list and immediately insert the title.

Usually, crashing a title means the company is falling far short of the revenue they need for a particular quarter, or an author failed to deliver a manuscript on time and they need to fill the void, or something of huge consequence happened around the world where the market is demanding a book. If you have a book selected to be the "crashee," then be aware of the situation and why it is happening.

Having a book crash any list is not necessarily a bad thing. For one, the title gets special attention from everyone. But as an author you do not have the time to develop relationships with those working on your book, and rather than having the eighteen to thirty-six months to prepare for the sale of your book, everything surrounding the publication of your book is accelerated. Typically, a crashed title is inserted in a list currently being sold, which means salespeople have to go back to the book buyers and resell that one title. Sometimes, depending on the title, it can be an advantage, and yet other times, a problem. Timing is everything.

The same questions apply to a crashed book as a focus title. Usually the circumstances are out of your control; there is little an author can do. Try to be aware of what is going on with your book at all times, ask questions and be willing to jump in on a minute's notice to help. Your willingness to throw yourself into the mix of an instant sale should be seen as a huge bonus for all involved.

HOW TO OVERCOME A BAD SALES HISTORY

If you have not been as successful in your publishing experience, all is not lost! You are most likely in need of a major re-positioning campaign for yourself and your book in-house or sometimes, depending upon the circumstance, with another publisher. Even though it is extremely difficult to overcome a bad sales history, there are ways to address the problem, no matter if it was your first or fifth book. However, you must be aware it is not easy and your chances at being successful are not as good. If you are an author struggling to get attention paid to your book and you find yourself in this situation, you need expert help.

You need to consult with an expert. Not an author, but someone who has gone through this many times and knows the marketplace. You need to strategize your position as an author by discussing your experience, your success and your failures and then devise a new way of getting yourself repositioned to become more successful. However, there are no guarantees and the competition is tremendous. To be successful in the publishing industry, you must have as much information about what goes on inside and understand how you can take advantage from the outside. If it is obvious your publisher has lost confidence in your ability to sell copies, then you best pull up stakes and move to another company. Don't waste your time trying to convince everyone in-house that mistakes in their marketing or distribution is the reason your book did not have a high sell-through. Take your experience, learn from it and move on. There are plenty of other publishers.

True Story of Repositioning

This is a perfect example of how to reposition an author. My former company signed a contract with a mass market paperback author who had recently left her previous publishing company because she was unhappy with her overall sales. Her third book was the first one we published by my company and the numbers came in well below what her previous publisher had been distributing. It was my job to convince her that the distribution on her third book was a positive step in the right direction and not a step back.

The author had left her old publisher because she wanted to grow in sales and she did not feel confident the publisher could do the job. Since we had a reputation as a publishing company that could take an existing author and make them a bestseller, she decided it was a good career move to sign with our company. The old company had a reputation for only wanting big numbers out the door and not caring about the sell-through percentage. So, with each successive book her gross number got bigger, but her net did not rise correspondingly. Thus, she was developing a history not leaving room for growth.

Selling an author with a downward trend is difficult at best. When we took her over, we repositioned her third book, stressing to the book buyers that she was a good writer whose previous titles had been published the wrong way. Her numbers (not actual, but modified to serve as an example) went something like this:

- First book published with the original company: 80,000 distributed with a net sale of 40,000 copies = 50% sell-through
- Second book also published with the original company: 100,000 distributed with a net of 45,000 copies = 45% sell-through
- Third book, new publisher: 70,000 distributed, net sale unknown.

As you can see, this author was averaging a net sale of around 42,500 copies on her first two books. Her first had a sell-through of 50%, which is respectable for a mass market paperback. However, her second book dropped to 45%, which is a trend in the wrong direction. The trend in net sales was a problem when her third book was being sold. So, to get the author back on track, her gross (total number distributed) needed to be reduced.

With an average of 42,500 net sales, a sales rep who is being reasonable with a book buyer will tell them that the 70,000 gross number should represent a 61% sell-through, based on the average net sale of the first two books. Depending upon the package, price and promotion, this new gross number gives the author a chance to grow and, hopefully, resurrect her career. What we did could easily have been done by the previous publisher. However, based on their reputation in the marketplace, the author needed a change.

The author was told why her gross number did not represent our inability to grow her as an author, even though it was ten thousand copies below her first book. After my meeting, she was not only pleased, but also excited we were looking out for her and actually taking the time to focus the distribution of her book to provide the highest possible sell-through percentage. Her previous publisher had never given her such an explanation.

It is hard to say why her second book did not sell through as well as or better than her first. I have no idea where her first two books were distributed, but it is possible the twenty thousand-copy increase from book one to book two resulted in an over-purchase by a few customers. In other words, her books may have been published in seasons when the company needed gross numbers to meet budget expectations and they used her books to gain that extra billing. How does that help an author? It doesn't. It actually hurts the author and damages her ability to continue writing and having her books bought.

Based on this story you might be wondering why my former company took the time and paid the attention to this book. After all, it seems contrary to everything I have written up to this point. The publisher paid little money when purchasing the rights to publish the author's third book and the only way to leverage a poor sell-through to a book buyer was to illustrate the people in sales are being smarter about how they publish her newest book. Generating revenue is still the most important item on the publisher's agenda and paying little for the rights to publish a mass market paperback able to generate an initial order of seventy thousand copies far exceeds what most authors can offer. So, in this situation it was a win-win for the author and her new publisher.

Three Years of Sales Records

Most major booksellers maintain detailed sales records for at least three years. Chances are that if you had a bad sell-through with a previous book older than three years, the sales history will have been destroyed. On the flip side, there might be some book buyers who remember a particular title and author. Regardless of the situation, any author willing to place themselves under the microscope for another shot at being a successful author needs to understand that overcoming any bad sales history is difficult, but not impossible.

Of course you can always write under another name, but know that every book you have written previously should be properly identified to a book buyer. This is part of the credibility of the sales rep and certainly the publishing company. A good rep should never hold back information from a book buyer that would prevent them from making a decision without all of the facts. This is a practice often ignored by some publishers. Either way, authors in a downward trend willing to take a risk should know it can be done!

Part 5

PARTICIPATE IN DECISIONS

As you begin your quest to become a published author, it is crucial you make every attempt to participate in as many decisions as possible surrounding the publication of your book. First, you need to educate yourself about the business, why decisions are made and how those decisions can impact the sale of your book. In order to take part, you must be willing and knowledgeable. If you lack either, you will not be successful.

From the day you speak with your first potential agent, and then eventually meet your new editor and become acquainted with people at your new publisher, it is important to communicate that you want to participate in the process of publishing your book. You don't want to be demanding, but you need to make this point: *You understand that a high sell-through is the key to success and you are willing to do everything you can to help your publisher sell books.* This approach will signal to your agent, editor and publisher that you want to work with them not only to help make decisions, but to help sell books. If you have any hesitation in making this one simple statement, then you need to be willing to accept whatever decisions they make for you and your book and accept that the results can be catastrophic.

Your Rights as an Author

One of the single biggest mistakes writers make is leaving all of the details of their book's publication to their publisher. This fact has always baffled me and can be a critical mistake that can negatively impact your career as an author. After a writer spends so much time and effort to create a manuscript, why on earth would they want to leave the important details to someone else, most especially their publisher? Given the fact publishers today have limited time and resources, your ability to make knowledgeable suggestions can be seen as a plus for you and your book.

As a writer and an author, you have every right to be a partner in the decision making process. This does not mean you will have the right of "first refusal." Your publisher will not allow you to make the final decision on anything. But you do want to be a part of the discussion and have the capability to make suggestions before a final decision is made. You should want to participate in the decisions and make every attempt to have a positive impact on your book's publication. You must make certain you can speak intelligently about the marketplace; otherwise, your ability to be a contributing factor will be diminished. Based on the skills you have developed and knowledge you've gained, you want to complement the publisher and assist in the distribution and sale of your book.

Granted, publishers publish thousands of books every year and it is certainly not practical, or even possible, for every author to work with their publisher on every book. Many authors do not want the responsibility. They see their job as writing and they do not want to be bothered with the other details. However, to walk away from the responsibility and then criticize when the book doesn't work will lead publishers and in-house staff to ignore the future wishes of that author.

Your Goals as an Author

Consider your goals and what you want out of your work. If you desire success in the marketplace, successful sales at retail, growing distribution and a lifetime of work as a writer, then I would strongly suggest you become a willing participant in the publishing process.

As with any endeavor in life, you have to earn the right to offer suggestions. What you want as an author is an opportunity to be a part of the process. You want to be able to provide suggestions and ideas. You want to contribute to the decision-making process before the final decision is made. But this will not happen if you do not have the knowledge to speak intelligently about your genre and the overall marketplace.

It's important from day one to express your willingness to be a participant. Your publisher will not allow you to be involved contractually in the decisions surrounding your book. Only the top-dollar authors have control over covers, prices, or anything else. What you do want to make clear is that your goal is a high sell-through and you would like the opportunity to offer suggestions surrounding your book based on the knowledge you have of the marketplace. You're only asking for the right to contribute to decisions and to have the opportunity to be a participant.

This, of course, presupposes you are prepared to play a role. If you are not willing to take part in everything and you end up giving ground too many times, you will forfeit other opportunities on other decisions. The key is whether or not your suggestions make sense when taking into consideration the marketplace and your knowledge of it.

Publishers are flooded with new titles every month, a necessary part of the business. Be ready to share control, do your part and allow them to do theirs. Leaving the final decisions to the experts is okay; just don't relinquish total control to the publisher. My suggestion is that you decide to become a willing and enthusiastic participant in the process of publishing your book.

Understand Your Market

Writers are typically readers. They read books on topics that interest them and books written by authors they enjoy. They should also be voracious readers in their genre. If you are a writer and do not read, especially within the category in which you write, then it would be wise to start. In addition to reading books in your competitive category, you should begin to notice the myriad ways a publisher markets and sell books. Become a regular visitor to your local bookstore, preferably an independent, and do not limit yourself to chain bookstores. The more you visit, the quicker you will begin to see the changes in the market. You will begin to understand what's going on and how books are being merchandised, marketed and sold. The bookstore is your laboratory. Visit and observe; the information you obtain will help you to speak intelligently about the business.

You can start by looking at the covers of a variety of books. Notice the colors and images. Does the publisher use drawings, photographs, or neither on the covers? Make note of the pricing within the category. What is the range? Are there sub-categories prominent within your genre? Are there exceptions?

Become aware of how the books are being merchandised. Are they spine out on the shelves or face out? How many copies are on the shelf? Where are the books being placed in the stores—on shelves, in cardboard floor displays, on smaller shelf displays, on tabletops? How are they being positioned on a table or in shelves? Where are the floor displays located within the store? Know where your category of books is found in the stores. This kind of information will serve as a foundation of your knowledge when you become a part of the process of successfully publishing your book.

Not only should you have a working knowledge of your own category, you should take a look at the store in general. Find out what books are on the bestseller lists, including fiction, non-fiction, hardcover and paperback. Observe how those books are being merchandised. What categories of books are being given prime display space? Are they only the current best-selling titles? If not, what other categories of books are getting prominent space in the store?

Check the prices of the best-selling titles. Make mental notes about their cover work, the images and the colors. Most importantly, how are the best-selling books being displayed? Remember the space inside a retail bookseller is prime real estate and it's for rent. However, store managers will not necessarily give that space to the highest bidder. Booksellers must maintain a balance between placement for space and the ability of a title to sell copies.

Speak Intelligently

You want to be able to discuss, in general terms, everything about books in your particular genre. You do that by visiting stores, making observations and reading lots of books. Publishers expect writers to be generally knowledgeable about editorial content, the editorial process and the academics of writing. They do not often encounter writers who have a keen awareness of pricing, cover art, book merchandising and displays. Knowing this will make you a more informed author and your publisher should see this as a big plus. This knowledge of the marketplace will also give you an advantage when it comes to decision time for your book.

You probably have a favorite bookstore you frequent. If it happens to be one of the big national chain stores, seek out a general independent bookstore, not one that offers only a narrow range of titles, such as a mystery-only store, but one that tries to give customers a broad range of titles and categories. Become acquainted with the store personnel, talk to them about books, ask what's selling and why. I've found these individuals are usually more than willing to talk with you since customers seldom ask their opinions on books. Your chances of finding a knowledgeable store employee are much better at an independent store than a chain store.

Notice where the independent store puts its new-author section. Again, give the category a once-over, noting everything about the books you can absorb. Also, note whether the books are offered in hardcover, trade paper or mass paper editions. Once you get the hang of all the merchandising and display elements for the books, begin to make observations across time. Notice the months of publication and the publishers. If a pattern begins to emerge in which you identify companies that seem to do a good job of publishing books in your genre, then these houses can be the focus of your search for the publisher who will eventually publish you successfully.

When a few publishers have begun to stand out, then ask the employees about those publishers. Find out the reputation of each company and what kinds of titles it publishes. If you are lucky, you may encounter the store's book buyer and you might be able to get your hands on one of the publisher's seasonal catalogs. Here you will find all kinds of good information on aspects of merchandising and marketing that would have taken you several trips to the store to discover. However, you cannot read a publisher's seasonal catalog and get the same information you can by visiting stores and making your own observations. Looking around a bookstore and browsing through a catalog are two different things. They both offer important information, but they are not interchangeable. The catalog will give you a sense of the mix of titles for a particular season for that publisher.

Publisher catalogs can be difficult to get your hands on because they can be expensive to print and sales reps usually only have a few extra each season. So it is rare that a company will give a store an extra seasonal catalog. If that's the case, maybe the buyer will let you browse the catalog while you sit in the store. Either way, the information can be valuable.

You Must Know Your Market

I hope I've helped you to see why knowing your market, having a feel for how books are being published and gaining general knowledge of the merchandising inside a bookstore will help you contribute to the decision-making process.

You want your book to be similar to, yet different from, others in your category. If all the titles have similarities, you can bet there is a reason. Publishers copy each other, but the consumers are the ones who make the final decisions on what to buy. If a certain color is not being used on any books within a category, then you must assume there are reasons. There are reasons for similarities and differences in the prices on books and their location within a store. Similar yet different sounds easy, doesn't it?

Can you find the book you are writing in the bookstore? If not, you might want to consider why. Publishers are risk averse, so seldom will they go out on a limb to try something completely new and different. Of course, that is only a general rule. Take my own book for example: there is nothing even close to it found on the shelves of the writing section in any bookstore. I know; I've checked. Finding books similar to the one you are writing will give you some direction when you begin the process of understanding your market.

Selling Yourself

From the time you sign the contract with your publisher, through the entire process of getting your book to the bookseller, you should be selling yourself to everyone up and down your ladder of contacts.

Usually, writers come across with a superior attitude, the attitude that their job is done and now it is up to the publisher to make their book a bestseller. This approach earns the writer zero points and the book ends up the same as all the others: just another title on the list.

However, if you approach the staff with a sense of gratitude and an appreciation for all their hard work, you and your book will begin to stand out from the rest. With your knowledge of the marketplace, knowing books in your genre and being capable of speaking intelligently about the business will go a long way. This is something you desperately need for your book to be successful.

From the beginning, you need to be seen in-house as a writer who really cares about what happens to your book and understands it is the hard work of everyone involved that will result in your book being successful. You need to be seen as an author who is informed about the process and is willing to go the extra mile for each department.

It is all in the approach and this is something anyone can do. You may think you have never sold a thing in your life, but you would be wrong. In one-way or another, you sell yourself every day. Consciously or unconsciously, you want to make a certain impression on people or gain specific results on a daily basis. In fact, you sell yourself to everyone with whom you come into contact. Succeeding is all about having a positive attitude.

There are three words that describe how you should treat everyone in-house: you should be honest, sincere and humble. You must always come across as valuing and practicing honesty and sincerity in your relationships and as having humility as a human being. If you can do this, then you can sell yourself. In selling yourself, you also sell your book and selling your book in-house can be as important as getting it sold at retail. One compliments the other. If your work fails in-house, it will most likely fail at retail.

Understand the Sales Force

It is important to understand some basic facts about the people who will be selling your book to booksellers. The sales group, above all others, can have the greatest impact on the success (or failure) of your book.

After all the in-house work is complete, the last people to handle your book are the ones who actually make the presentation to the book buyers; they are the sales representatives and national account managers. These people are critical to your book's success. But a publisher's sales reps scattered around the country are among the ones who receive the least amount of attention and typically get the most grief (failure of a book to sell always rolls downhill). They also happen to be some of the lowest paid employees of the publishing company.

Due to the size of the booksellers they handle, national account managers based outside of New York get more attention than the sales reps, but also get a lot more grief.

You must understand the individuals at the local levels as well as the national account people in the field (selling your book to the local stores and to the smaller national accounts) can have an enormous impact on the success of your book. Often overlooked, the sales force outside of New York can be key to getting your book published successfully. These are the folks who make the presentations to the book buyers who ultimately determine what distribution your book receives out in the marketplace.

For most of the local reps and some of the national account reps, their priorities go something like this: family, health, home, church, friends, hobbies and somewhere way down the line comes their job and selling books. Remember, your priorities and their priorities are not the same.

These folks need a reason to pay attention to any one particular book. The best way to accomplish this is by personalizing your book. Try to make your book special by turning yourself into a real person to them, someone who cares about the difficulty of the sales rep's job; someone willing to help. You need to offer yourself in any way that will help make your book a success. You do this by being honest, sincere and humble in any and all communication and by making the sales force believe you want to work *with* them, instead of expecting them to work for you.

The Sales Reps

Territories for the local sales reps have gotten larger over the years. As companies have downsized, the numbers of reps have dropped. They are usually the first to go when the budgets don't work. The number of accounts a typical sales rep calls on has increased, the amount of travel time away from their families has increased, and the amount of paperwork continues to grow. The rep's job has gotten a lot tougher and definitely more demanding.

These people sell hundreds of titles a year. Most of these salespeople have been around for years. They understand the business, they know how things work and they know how to get things done. Sales representatives can be your biggest assets if you make them feel respected and appreciated.

You must go into the publishing process with a clear understanding that the people you'll typically deal with the least are the ones who can have the biggest impact on the success of your book. Once you have decided to be a participant in the decisions surrounding the publication of your book and you are selling yourself every step along the way, your approach will serve you well in your dealings with the sales group and will pay off in big ways. Certainly it's important to make contacts in-house and maintain good relationships with all departments, but don't forget about those who are selling books in territories around the U.S. You need their support as much as you need anyone's, if not more.

Agents and Contracts

Finding the right agent and negotiating the contract are well beyond the scope of this writing. You would be wise to find other sources of information on these topics. However, there are suggestions I can offer in both areas. These tips come from authors with whom I have worked over the years.

First, to find the right agent you must talk to others who have gone through the same process. I cannot stress this enough. Your agent is critical. He or she can mold your book and impact how the publisher deals with you in every respect, long before you have a chance to be charming. It is important you talk to a variety of people before selecting an agent.

Agents have reputations within the industry, just like anyone else. If you belong to a writers group, which includes published authors, they can be a great source of information. If you belong to a national author organization, then you should utilize that resource to gather information about agents. If you do not belong to a local or national group, then seek one out, either through your local independent bookstore or by searching the web.

Another potential source of information are freelance editor groups who may meet at your local bookstore. Contacting them may yield some good information on agents. You want to get a list of agents and the authors they represent. Then see if you can find their books in stores. If you can't, you have to ask yourself why you can't.

Go about finding an agent the same way you would select anything important. Do your homework. Talk to as many people as you can, gather as much information as possible and make a list of candidates. Once you get your facts together, you should interview each potential agent on your list. Yes, this process is exhausting, but more than likely the really good agents will appreciate your thoroughness. After all, they are looking for talent, for writers whom they can sell to a publisher. If you have confidence in your ability then don't be shy about going for the best agents.

If you end up with an agent who was not the first one on your list but who seems eager to get your career going, fear not. The agent is going to make your introductions to publishers. You have an idea of who you want to publish your work after all the homework you have done in the bookstores. However, if your agent tries to deflect those publishers, for whatever reason, ask questions and find out why. If you don't like the answers, then perhaps you need to start the agent search over again.

If the agent convinces you to go with a publisher other than those on your list, you need to do your homework and find out all you can about that company. Find out everything about what the house publishes and how they do business. Even if you have to settle for an agent who wasn't your first pick and a publisher not on your list, you can still get your book published successfully.

When contract time rolls around, again, do your homework. Ask lots of people lots of questions. Gather all the relevant facts and use them to your advantage. Have the contract read by your own outside legal counsel. You might be surprised at how many new authors skip this step. They are so excited by the idea of getting published they let the agent convince them the contract is a "standard" one for all publishing houses. Get your attorney to look the contract over. When he or she does, make sure you are comfortable with everything and that it meets your goals as an author.

Remember, you are separating yourself from all the other authors by being more informed about the process. You have educated yourself on the market, have a basic understanding of what goes on behind the scenes and all this knowledge can only empower you in your quest to be published successfully.

HOW TO MAKE SUGGESTIONS

Now you will put all those facts you gathered to use. Remember, as a new author you are not going to have final cover approval or final say in other important matters. Those perks are given only to the big-money authors. However, you should be allowed to be part of the decision-making process. Before any decisions are made about your book, regarding the price, cover, artwork, category and so forth, ask to be part of the process and to be informed of the how's and why's of the publisher's decisions.

Their first reaction will probably be to tell you to go jump off a bridge. But if you explain that your goal is to contribute in a positive way, you want to do everything you can to help them sell books and you can convince them you have a working knowledge of the marketplace, you have a real chance of making this happen. That doesn't mean they are going to allow you to sit in on the meetings, but you should get an opportunity to ask questions and make suggestions.

Being a Keen Observer

Being a keen observer of the marketplace will allow you to speak intelligently about your market. This will help you make valuable suggestions before decisions are finalized. If you see some competitive covers you like, give copies to your editor to be used as suggestions. You can do the same with prices and, at the proper time, promotions, publicity and so on. Remember, all you want is the opportunity to make suggestions regarding the publication of a book you may have spent years writing.

Timing—when you get to ask those questions and make your suggestions—is critical. For example, if the house decides on a jacket for your book and you do not have the opportunity to ask questions or make suggestions until three weeks later, then, most likely, your cover will have been put to bed and your chance of having a suggestion heard, let alone have changes made, will have passed. You must depend on your editor to get you in the loop before decisions are being made and you need to make suggestions.

The likelihood of a new author asking questions or making suggestions that will actually lead to changes is not as slim as you may think. The fact that you know the questions to ask will send a signal that you are aware of your market. That information will travel fast throughout the company, because it is unusual an author has a genuine working knowledge of the marketplace. The result will be that people will think twice before they make haphazard decisions about your book and they will be more likely to listen to your suggestions. This is especially important when it comes to the decisions about numbers.

Even if your publisher absolutely refuses to allow you to be part of the decision-making process and is unwilling to allow you to offer suggestions, there are ways to do just that and get your point across. Suppose this is your plight: you did not get the agent you wanted or the publisher you wanted and now you find they won't even allow you to be a partner in the process. How do you get your book published successfully? You go directly to the sales and marketing departments and plead your case, making certain they understand that all you want to do is help them sell books and your goal is a distribution with a high percent of sale. This will only be possible if you have made contact with them earlier along in the process and approached them as an author who is honest, sincere and humble.

Test Your Editor

If you thought you had little choice selecting your agent or publisher, you have even less choice of your new editor. When the agent introduces your book to the house, the person the agent has contact with will most likely be an editor. This depends on the agent's stature; some well-known agents go directly to the publishers of the various imprints, maybe even to the CEO of the company, to make an introduction for a writer. However, most often, agents will go to editors, or even assistant editors.

The editor should be someone who works exclusively in the category of your book. If you are writing mysteries, your agent should not be introducing you to an editor who specializes in military history (unless that introduction is part of a roundabout process and will eventually get you to the right editor).

It is important you ask your agent for the name of any editor to whom you are being introduced prior to your first meeting. You'll want to ask that editor for a list of books they've edited. From your friend at the local independent bookstore, find out how these books sold (net copies at retail). Aside from how they sold, how long ago were they published? Find out the pub dates for their books. If the editor is not working with authors who have current titles in stores, this could signal a potential problem and you should ask why.

In addition to how the editor's books sold, find out whether the books were ever reordered. Any book that sells well enough should have been reordered (for the store to replenish the inventory). This is only one small slice of the retail sales pie, but it should give you an idea of the editor's success. You should also visit the larger chain bookstores to find out if any of the authors have books in these stores. If not, you should hear alarm bells going off in your head.

Suppose you have a new editor and you get along splendidly. You are happy. Your dreams are coming true. Now it is time to begin developing relationships with the in-house people who will be working on your book. Ask your editor to introduce you to them as early after you've signed your contract as possible. This gives you plenty of time to establish relationships.

When you ask your editor to make these introductions, do not be specific. Instead, simply ask to meet those working on your book. Ask to meet people in the advertising, publicity, art, editorial and, of course, sales and marketing departments. Do not request department heads, because it is doubtful that will happen. You need to find where your editor stands within the company and the only way to do that is to make a general request and see who comes to the table. Your new editor will invite those who he or she is most comfortable with. Whether or not you get to meet the heads of departments will tell you something about your editor's stature within the company. It's possible the key individuals are not available and you will find that out at the meeting.

Visit Your Publisher

Assuming you do not live in New York, you will need to make a trip to Manhattan at some point to meet your in-house contacts (if your publisher is not based in New York, then you are not being published by what I call a major trade company). That's okay, everything is relevant to you as an author and it really doesn't matter where your publisher's corporate offices are located. Good publishers are found across the country.

Lunch meetings are a big part of New York publishing, so if your meeting takes place somewhere else you are beginning to see where you and your editor are in the pecking order at your new publisher. But, don't worry, if your meetings are not over lunch (which can be long and boring) you can get just as much accomplished in the offices as you can at a restaurant in midtown Manhattan.

Never, ever, share too much information with anyone in-house about what you have discovered by being a regular visitor to your local independent bookstore. Your knowledge will come across naturally as you develop your relationships within each department and as you offer suggestions. You will have ample time to show the company just how much you know.

Publishers and in-house folks avoid authors who come across as know-it-alls.

Similarly, if you covey an attitude of being superior to those laboring within the company, you will hurt your chances of being successful. If you come across as too accommodating or someone looking for a favor or who flatters everyone, your boat will sink. Keep your cards close to the vest. When your new friends make industry comments, just ask them questions and do not pretend to have the answers; certainly do not tell them they are wrong. Their answers to your questions will tell you if they are blowing smoke or if they really know their stuff. Remember: The best policy is to be honest, sincere and humble.

Learn Job Titles and Responsibilities

You may find that your editor introduces you to assistants or to assistants of other assistants. In this case you will have a more difficult time getting to the decision makers. If your editor does not introduce you to anyone in the sales department, you will have to find a way to make these contacts happen, but at this point do not force the issue.

Consider the meeting as part of your preparation to have your book successfully published. Being introduced to the people who will be working on your book and developing positive relationships with them is important. Even if they end up being assistants to other assistants, get their business cards. When you get home, make sure you write and thank them for their time and tell them you are looking forward to working with them. Upon the foundation of your relationships with these people you will start building other relationships. Your first contacts can introduce you to those who really make decisions. These people become your springboard.

You build solid relationships in a publishing house by making people feel important, making them feel like experts in the publishing world and getting them to share their knowledge. As you build these relationships you will learn whether these particular individuals are really important to your goal of being published successfully. If not, continue to be nice, but subtly move up the chain of command. Eventually, you want to become acquainted with the head of each department, or at least his or her right- hand person. In addition, somewhere along the line, you want to meet some of the key salespeople. This area is where you need to have a real impact.

Use your keen sense and people skills to gather information about the employees, their jobs and importance within the company. You are not using them; you are merely being nice and working your way to the most important people, the decision makers.

MEET THE SALES GROUP

At this point you have done your homework. You know your category, competitive titles and authors. You have a grasp of how books are merchandised and marketed, packaged and priced. You have an agent and a publisher. They may not have been your first choices, but they give you a place to start. Your editor may be working his or her way up the ladder and is currently little more than a glorified assistant trying to gain full-time editor status. You may have had little success meeting department heads because your editor only introduced you to assistants of assistants. Frustrated? Perhaps, but remember you still have an advantage over other authors. You have a better working knowledge about the world of publishing than most, thanks to your bookstore observations, and this will help you tremendously as you move forward. (Let me remind you again: Do not be too anxious to share what you know. Let your knowledge emerge as the publishing process continues.)

Don't Underestimate the Impact

At this point, you have been signed and your manuscript has been edited and scheduled for publication. More than likely, your pub date is far enough out that you have time to develop relationships with the in-house departments. You will be talking with your contacts to develop and deepen those relationships. As you do so, you would be wise to focus most of your effort where it will have the greatest impact. The key groups of people you must develop a relationship with, above all others, are the sales and marketing departments.

Let me anticipate your concerns before you begin to question the importance I place on the sales and marketing departments. Yes, I come from a sales background and, yes, I may be according the department more power than most of your fellow writers do, but in fact this is where authors make some of the biggest mistakes when dealing with their publishers. They underestimate the influence of the sales and marketing departments in determining the success of their book. Forget what you might have heard to the contrary. I've been there!

Everything up to this point in the life of your book has been a team effort. The art department created a great cover and advertising is doing all they can with the budget they have been given. Promotion for your book is in place and publicity has a plan for generating a buzz that should raise some eyebrows. This is all well and good. Great start. Now the ball is being handed over to the sales and marketing group.

This is a crucial time in your book's publishing life. If you haven't met the head of sales and marketing, do so now. If you have been unsuccessful in meeting anyone at a management level, then you will have to start at the bottom by trying to meet your local sales representative. You can work through your editor for this information, but if your department introductions yielded less than encouraging results then perhaps you want to look elsewhere. Your friend at the local independent bookstore should have the name and e-mail address of their local sales representative for your publisher.

If you get a sales rep's name from your local bookstore and that person is based in New York and you live several hundred miles from Manhattan, then more than likely the telemarketing department is servicing your store. If this is the case, then you will have to ask your editor to introduce you to someone in the sales department other than a member of the telemarketing group. That request will probably go to the head of the sales and marketing department and then will be handed off to someone in a much lower position.

If your editor is confused about the difference between the telemarketing group and sales and marketing, then your editor is completely out of the loop. The telephone sales staff handles those stores located in remote geographical areas or are so small in terms of net dollars sold that it does not pay for the company to have an actual territorial sales rep handle the account in person. If your local store falls into one of those two categories, that's fine for gathering information about your market and making other observations, but not for introducing you to the sales department. If this is the case, you must go to your editor and ask for another name and e-mail address in the sales department.

Starting Point

If you were not introduced to anyone inside the sales and marketing departments during your visit to the corporate office, start by sending an e-mail and ask to speak on the phone for a few minutes with someone in a management position. This will, of course, send all kinds of wrong signals, but someone will be obligated to speak to you.

At this point, ideally from your first meeting, you will be known in-house as an author who really cares about how your book is published. Not someone who is looking for special favors, but one who is honest, sincere and humble, all the things we talked about earlier.

Be aware that salespeople are seldom asked to call an author and on those rare occasions when they are asked to do so, it typically spells trouble. Generally, either the author is complaining that he cannot find his book at any local stores, or he is upset because a competing author got better shelf placement or positioning at an airport. So, when the sales department gets your request, they will likely respond with a built-in aversion to contacting you. But you will have worked to build a reputation that will help defuse that response. Your knowledge of the industry and how books are published will have been mentioned at meetings. Hence your phone call should not be something the department will be concerned about or try to avoid.

Now that you have a salesperson, hopefully a manager, on the phone, find out her position of responsibility with the company and start a conversation by making an assurance that your goal is a high sell-through and you are willing to do whatever is necessary to help sell books. Remember, your goal is not to question the person or put her on the spot, but to assure her that your desire is to help and nothing else.

Eventually this approach will pay huge dividends.

Know the Key Decision Makers

Within the sales department are factions that compete in-house for any number of things. There are the national account people who handle the really big customers and they usually outnumber the rest of the sales group. Then there are the field sales folks who deal with all the other booksellers, such as independent bookstores and distributors around the country.

In-house competition can range from getting the hottest author for the next tour, to getting books shipped to their accounts first when the print order runs low. (This happens when a book is selling well at retail and the company needs to allocate the remaining stock on hand prior to the receipt of the next reprint.) They also compete for rare resources, such as support staff, cooperative-advertising monies, additional marketing supplies and materials and anything else under the sun a sales force needs to operate.

It is not uncommon to find the head of sales is someone who does not have a direct background in sales. In other words, it can be someone who has never actually handled an account or sold in a territory. Similarly the head of marketing (who typically reports to the head of sales) will probably not have any formal training in marketing. These executives are often people who started at a low level in the company and worked their way up through the ranks. While this is quite noble and can speak well for the company, it does not bode well for the fortunes of the publisher, lacking management diversity that might help them grow.

This is information you must keep in mind as you begin to build your relationship within the sales and marketing departments. Understand where these people are coming from, the pressures of their jobs, their need to meet budgets. So when they have to talk with an author it would serve you well to convey your message simply, practice honesty, sincerity and humbleness. Remember, you want to be seen as someone who can help sell books. Your goal is a good distribution that gives you the best chance at a high sell-through. Salespeople appreciate this message, work with them and they will respond.

Understand the Numbers

Numbers and your understanding of them are important so I want to review the critical points again. The announced first print of your book is important only because it is derived from the budget number, which sets the stage for how the sales group will handle your book. The announced first print is based solely on the budget number given to your book. In most cases, it is selected to get the attention of the book buyer. Some book buyers will not take any book seriously unless the announced first print is one hundred thousand or more. The book buyers can then assume the book will get a minimum first printing of around sixty thousand copies. In fact, the actual first print and distribution number may be far less.

So why not give every book an announced first print of one hundred thousand? Because buyers will fail to take the numbers seriously. Eventually the publisher's credibility may be damaged. Announced first prints, on any list, can range from two-and-a-half million down to as low as ten thousand and anywhere in between.

Remember, the announced first print number means nothing in real terms. Book buyers look at that number to get an idea whether the title is one they should even consider. An announced first print number that is too low can place your book in a precarious position and damage your chances of being published successfully. You want a number that implies your book will have some basis of support. This level of support is what you need to discover in one of your eventual conversations with the sales manager.

For all the talk about announced first prints, actual first print numbers and budget numbers, the distribution number is actually the key to your success. You can have an announced first print number of one hundred thousand and an actual first print number of sixty thousand with a budget of sixty-five thousand and get a distribution of fifty thousand. All this seems fabulous on the surface. But the important question is, where are the fifty thousand copies being distributed? This is the most crucial question, above all the rest, and its answer is as elusive as any you've tried to get during your time with your publisher.

In all my years working at the management level of a major New York-based trade publisher, never has an author or agent asked me where their book was being distributed. That is because agents and authors tend to look at the overall number as being the key, when in fact a book getting a distribution of twenty-five thousand, compared to fifty thousand, can have a better chance of being published successfully simply because the distribution is better.

Booksellers Understand Distribution

Retailers break their stores down into categories. For the sake of discussion, let's say they label them A, B, or C-stores (A stores would be the largest format for the retail chain, B stores the mid-range store and C the smaller stores). Typically, the system is much more sophisticated, but for discussion purposes let's use these three labels. The bookseller will know what types of books sell in what stores and which categories sell best in which parts of the country. A buyer's purchases should reflect that bookseller's ability to sell your book at the highest sell-through percentage.

Publisher sales representatives have numbers that need to be met and so they try for the largest distribution number possible. That might not be the best scenario for your book. The largest distribution number, which looks good for the sales representative and looks good for the editor and agent, could mean disaster for you, the author, because the distribution will not necessarily give your book the best opportunity to sell through at retail.

After you have established a good working relationship within the sales department and they recognize you as an author whose only goal is a high sell-through, subsequent communication can focus on numbers. When those conversations begin, let the person give you all the announced numbers he wants. What you eventually want to know is how many copies of your book are actually being distributed into the marketplace and where they are going. Ask what the breakdown is of booksellers getting your book. In other words, how many bookstores, how many jobbers, how many discount retailers and wholesale clubs? These are the really important questions. The answers are the key to successful publishing with a high percent of sale.

Distribution is Key

Success is never about how many copies a publisher prints, or even announces they are going to print, but about how many copies are being mindfully distributed to the right booksellers, plain and simple! Good distribution should result in high sell-through percentages, which result in even bigger numbers on subsequent books and this, eventually, leads to growth as an author. Growth in net sales means you have been successfully published and that you have a solid career ahead.

PUBLISHERS AND DISTRIBUTORS

Up to this point, we've assumed your book is being published by one of the large trade houses based in New York. Even if your publisher is not one of the biggest and is not based in New York, your situation as an author is the same. The marketplace, booksellers, book buyers, the numbers are the same, regardless of the size of your publisher or where it is headquartered.

The biggest trade publishers with headquarters in New York typically have their own dedicated sales forces, meaning they publish, market and sell the books all through in-house staff. The company employs everyone involved. However, there are many publishers based in New York and elsewhere that depend on distributors to sell their books to booksellers. The company may not be able to afford its own dedicated sales group, so it contracts with a national distributor to sell its seasonal titles to booksellers. If your publisher sells through a distributor, your job of successfully publishing your book may be more difficult, depending on the distributor.

It's Still a Relationship Business

National distributors are companies that contract with a wide variety of small and medium-sized publishers to sell and distribute their books. These national distributors are representatives of small and medium sized publishers whose job it is to sell each company's seasonal titles around the country. These distributors represent many lines of books, some that are strikingly similar and others that fill a niche market. The publishers send their printed books to the warehouse of the distributor rather than directly to the bookseller. The distributor, in turn, controls and manages sales and shipment of the books to booksellers.

Distributors have a history of being paid in two different ways. One method used to be based entirely on the gross number of copies actually distributed to booksellers. The other is based on the total number of net copies sold by the booksellers. Gross copy payments resulted in excessive units being shipped and poor distribution, which meant poor sell-through percentages and this is why they are all but extinct. The net copy method is better for the publisher and certainly the author.

Since the distributor does not work directly for the publisher, there are now two companies, with two different sales contacts, with whom you need to build relationships. Making it even more complicated, an editor of a publishing company rarely has any contact with a national distributor. This will make getting answers much more difficult for you.

Distribution is the key. Everything you have read to this point is the same whether you are dealing with a national distributor or publisher. However, if your publisher is using a national distributor, this introduces additional factors that can affect your book. How your publisher's books are sold and distributed is one factor you need to consider when you sign a contract and it is an issue you need to resolve with your agent. If you have doubts about the publisher or its distributors go to your local bookstore, ask to speak with the book buyer and express your concerns. All the buyer can do is explain the industry reputation of the distributor and publisher, which will give you information to make a more informed decision about where you want your book published.

If your publisher does not have its own in-house sales group, the company will have someone who acts as a liaison to the national distributor and this is the person with whom you need to develop a relationship. Ideally, this person will have a solid reputation with the distributor. You should try to meet with both the liaison and the key management person at the distributor to convey both your hopes and your concerns about your book's distribution.

Ask the same questions of the distributor as you would anyone in-house. Numbers can be used to "explain" anything, but with your understanding of distribution and how important it is to your book, you should be able to elicit some straight answers from the distributor. If nothing else, you will have separated yourself as an author and elevated your book above all the rest.

Some very small publishers use outside commission sales reps to sell their titles around the country. The process is identical to that of the publisher or distributor. Ask the same questions, outline your goals as an author and maintain a relationship with management. It's your book, your life's work; so protect yourself as an author.

A BAD EXAMPLE

At this point you are probably thinking to yourself that everything you have read thus far about building in-house relationships is simple common sense and decency. The reason I have taken time to outline such basic, commonsense characteristics is that, in my experience, these traits were rare among the authors who dealt with my sales group. I am not drawing a generalization about authors. I'm just describing my personal experience with authors with whom I came into contact over the course of many years. Let me give you a bad example.

What Not To Do

The setting was a meeting held in New York that included several of the national account people and sales managers from my company. We were sitting in a boardroom around a large oval table. In the middle of our morning session, the CEO of our company walked in with a stern look on his face. It was not a good sign.

It was not unusual for our CEO to interrupt a meeting for anything that might have caught his attention, but the look told us something wasn't right, so we prepared ourselves. He sat down and told us that an author and his agent were outside the boardroom and they wanted to speak with us about a problem.

Now, it was not unusual for an author to want to meet everyone. Typically, such an introduction amounted to nothing more than a casual handshake and a brief introduction; then the author would thank us for our work and go on his way, leaving us to our meeting.

On this occasion, the author who wanted to speak with us had written several books, a couple having made various bestseller lists around the country. He is a well-known author whose face would be easily recognized. His most current book had started slowly and was not selling like his previous titles. The fact that he and his agent wanted to speak with us could not be good.

When they entered the room, the author and agent were dressed like they were ready to step in front of a camera and everyone was all smiles, but when asked if they wanted to go around the room for introductions they passed on the opportunity—another bad sign. They wanted to get down to business and quickly.

The author began by telling the group what a horrible job we had done in selling his latest book. Not only was he terribly disappointed, but he also wanted us to know that neither he nor "his people" could find copies in stores around the country. He demanded to know why. He would name a city and large retail chain store without giving details.

You see, when an author makes such a general statement, listing cities and stores without being specific as to the individual location, there is no way a salesperson can answer with any specificity. Each chain can have a number of stores in various cities and there can be any number of reasons why an author fails to find copies in a particular store. For a man who was a best-selling author and obviously well educated, to make such a broad statement was ridiculous.

Well, everyone was dumbfounded that an author would come into a room full of the very people who can make or break his book and make such outrageous statements. Even more surprising, and certainly disappointing, was the fact our CEO allowed an author and agent to make those statements to the company's top salespeople.

Immediately, our boss began to tap dance around everything but the truth, hoping to find an area where he could spread enough bull to make the answer plausible. The author was not buying any of it. The agent told us we were the bottom of the barrel when it came to sales ability, because based on his experience with large trade publishers any of those other groups would have been able to distribute far more copies of his author's book than we had.

So, there we sat while an author and his agent blasted the entire group for doing a lousy job with his recent book. Forget the fact we had helped make two of his previous titles national bestsellers. Suddenly, the author's cell phone rang; "his people" were calling from around the country to report they could not find copies of his book. What a gigantic mistake!

You would think common sense and decency would have told this fellow that criticizing the sales force and doing so in such a blatant and demeaning manner would not get the reaction he wanted. Well, he got zero action. In fact, this book tanked. His next book got even less in up-front distribution and suffered more in net sales than any of his previous books. Talk about a good way to kill a writing career.

Sometimes what seems obvious is not obvious for some people. Again, I'm not drawing generalizations about authors, just trying to make it as clear as possible. Regarding your book, you must treat everyone with common sense and decency. Be honest, sincere and humble. If you don't, these folks behind the scenes can kill your book and career.

WHATEVER IT TAKES

Above all else, it is absolutely essential you do two things to give your book a better chance at being published successfully: (1) find a way to get your book recognized in-house and (2) understand that success depends on being knowledgeable about the marketplace and speaking intelligently about the business of publishing.

Thus, before your book is published, there are two areas where you need to focus your attention. The first is in-house and the second is the retail marketplace. The in-house part of this equation has already been covered; now let's talk briefly about the retail level.

Be Realistic

The region of the country where you live is the place to start. You should have become acquainted with the staff at your local bookstore, perhaps the book buyer and maybe even the owner. Now that you are going to be published, take them out to lunch and pick their brains. Tell them you would like their ideas on how to get some regional attention drawn to your book at all the independent bookstores in surrounding states. Whether you use their ideas or not, you will be building a positive relationship you can count on later.

When your publisher lets you know how much money the company is willing to spend to support your book, you need to have an idea of where to suggest they spend those dollars. Your best chance at getting the kind of distribution you need, to achieve the highest sell-through, would more than likely be on a regional basis. A regional presence, preferably in the area where you live, would make perfect sense and should make it easier to get publicity.

Know Where to Focus

Focus on the independent bookstores in your region and suggest the publisher spend its money to promote your book in those areas. There are any number of things you can do. For example, from a publicity standpoint, try for local newspaper interviews. From an advertising standpoint, ask for bookmarks to be placed in the stores prior to publication. The possibilities are endless.

Whatever you decide, do not leave this up to the publisher. You must make suggestions to them on how to spend their money. Back when you were in the bookstore gathering information and learning your market, you probably noticed a variety of promotional gimmicks publishers were using to promote books. Now is the time to use those ideas for your book. Remember, there is nothing new in this area, everyone copies everyone else so when something catches your eye, don't be afraid to use the idea for yourself.

Once your publisher agrees that a regional focus would work, you must make certain the distribution for your book has a strong spread among regional booksellers. This is common sense, right? But do not take it for granted. What has become obvious to you may not be as obvious to a sales group handling several hundred titles.

Success May Cost You

If it takes some time and money out of your own pocket to visit stores in your part of the country, then do whatever it takes! In the early days of my career it was not unusual to see authors driving around the country to visit booksellers. This happened all the time. Today, you rarely see authors taking the time, or spending their own money, to visit booksellers; at least, the authors at my former employer did not do that sort of thing.If you start with a regional presence and build sales around that customer base, you can then expand to other parts of the country and other groups of booksellers. Building sales by establishing a clear regional focus for your book and letting the publisher know how you want to advertise and promote, will help you become a successful author.

There are No Guarantees

Your book can have the best jacket, the lowest price, the greatest promotion and publicity schedule, fabulous advertising, the most wonderful heartwarming story in the world, with the most tightly focused distribution ever and still not sell.

This is the way of the publishing world, or any world where the decisions of consumers remain the ultimate test. If there were someone who could identify, beyond a doubt, what books or products would and would not sell, this person would not only be a genius of some magnitude, but, more than likely, the richest person in the universe. The fact is, no one knows. You can have the latest sales data, the best information and the best instincts and judgment and the product may still not move off the shelf.

Whether a book will sell depends on a wide variety of factors. Timing is critical. Successful books often have some sort of positive timing involved. For example, in one of my early years in the business the company I worked for at the time published a pseudo-biography of Elvis Presley, written by someone who had supposedly worked with him for years. The book got minimal distribution. It just so happened the book was initially distributed the month Elvis died and it went on to sell a few million copies.

One day, while working in the New York office, I got a call from the publisher about a book we had held back: a biography of Sammy Davis, Jr. The boss wanted to hold it until his death, which at the time was imminent. The publisher had heard a news report that Sammy was close to death, so he wanted me to get the troops going and sell that book. As horrible as it sounds, what do you think editors were doing the day after 9/11? Calling agents for anything written on terrorism. An example of how publishers will do anything to leverage the timing on a book.

Another critical element is word of mouth. I had the opportunity to work with one of the most successful hardcover books ever. It was a book with a simple story, clever and cute but didn't have that "wow" appeal some manuscripts have when circulated in-house. Touching story, yes, but not something anyone thought would end up selling several million copies.

The book was initially distributed in modest numbers. Then one day a single independent bookseller started to spread the word about how his customers just loved this book. After months of steady sales, we started to see larger increases and they kept building month after month.

As word spread across a larger part of the country, we could sense something was happening. The reorders kept building, the publicity started to gain momentum and after a period of many, many months, the book finally hit the national bestseller lists, starting at the bottom. Then it began to climb and we never looked back.

The book stayed at the top of the bestseller lists for months and eventually it sold over seven million hardcover copies. It became a major motion picture and the sales continued. It was quite a ride and fun to be a part of that book's success. The book was *The Bridges of Madison County* written by Robert James Waller.

The point being, sometimes books take time, sometimes a lot of time, to build sales. If you believe in your book, then be willing to put your efforts toward getting it properly distributed and eventually sold. However, you also need to recognize when to move on to the next book. You can always have hope, but be smart enough to know when a book has run its course. At that point, it is not doing anyone any good to try to force out more copies.

No One Here Gets Out Alive

The period right before Christmas at a publishing house is relatively quiet. Retailers are scrambling to make every sale and the last thing they want is to hear from a salesperson. So, there is about a two-week down time before the holiday season. This gives everyone in-house a chance to get caught up and ready for the budget race that begins the first day back to work after the New Year.

During what turned out to be my last Christmas holiday working in New York, my boss asked everyone to come up with his or her favorite backlist title of all time. We were asked to find a copy of the book or the cover and bring it to the next meeting. My choice was an old title that sold extremely well and continued to backlist: *No One Here Gets Out Alive*, Written by Jerry Hopkins and Danny Sugarman. It is the story of Jim Morrison and The Doors.

Little did I realize that my boss, tongue in cheek, would take exception to my selection, suggesting perhaps there was a message behind my choice of backlist titles. Two months later I decided it was time for my twenty-plus years inside the world of New York publishing to come to an end. That cover hangs above my desk now to remind me why I left. It has also provided me with a bit of inspiration from time to time.

Publishers are not in the business to lose money. They want to make money and they *must* make money. The result is that 90% of the titles published each season represent less than 10% of the billing. If you are the author of one of those 90%, you need to find a way to separate yourself from the pack.

For any new writer who wants to become an author and for those authors who are looking to find a new path to success, it can be elusive; you must have the information to overcome the obstacles that confront you. For writers who enter the publishing arena with little more than hope and a great manuscript, the title of my all-time favorite backlist book probably describes your chances: *No One Here Gets Out Alive.*

CONCLUSION

Here you have a broad overview of the publishing business and suggestions on how you can get your book successfully published. This information will help you make informed decisions about the publication of your book.

My years in the business were exciting. I had the opportunity to meet many talented and wonderful people. I would not trade that experience for anything. I also hope that sharing my experience will give you the help you need to make your dream come true. Information is like pieces of a puzzle; it's great if you know what to do with it and how to use it to your advantage.

I want to leave you with a story about my first author tour. At the time, I was a new sales rep working a territory that included four states. One day, I got a call from my boss telling me one of our biggest and best paperback authors would be touring and it was my responsibility to escort her and her husband around a city many miles from my home.

Since I had only visited the city a couple times, I had to leave early, find a city map and learn my way around so I could feel sure everything would go smoothly and without incident. So, I received the itinerary and tour schedule with the key contact information and headed off to my destination.

The first morning of the tour, the author was scheduled for a television interview at a downtown location. Having driven the route the previous day, I had a good idea about the time we should leave the hotel, allowing for traffic and unforeseen problems. We arrived at the station with time to spare. I dropped the author and her husband off at the front door and proceeded to find a parking spot. A parking garage was my only choice.

After parking, I took my time walking the two blocks to the television station. When I walked in the door the receptionist asked if she could help me and I told her yes, I was accompanying an author to be interviewed for the morning show. The lady smiled and said, "You are the second person this morning who's asked about that show, but it's broadcast from the other station in town."

Well, I must have turned seven shades of red and my jaw dropped several inches. Panic quickly set in. I checked my itinerary and was a bit relieved to see the name of the show was correct, but the location and name of the television station were wrong. Okay, someone else had screwed up, but it was still my problem because I had an author walking the streets scheduled for a television interview in a few minutes.

After taking a certain delight in my predicament, the receptionist told me the correct station was only a few blocks away and she had given directions to the author and her husband when they arrived. I fled as fast as I could to the right location and waited.

After what seemed like hours, the author emerged with her husband and smiled broadly and joked, "What a way to start the day." I was speechless, but relieved. The author was not only kind about the whole incident, she assured me mistakes happen all the time and I was not to worry.

The day had not started off on the right foot, but it was far from over. Next she had a book signing at a large bookseller who happened to be a mass merchant. When we arrived, the store was not ready for us even though they had known we were coming. There was no place to sit and no table where the author could sign books. Fortunately, plenty of copies were available, just nowhere to set up the signing.

After a few minutes of scrambling, the store managed to create a spot, stack the books and get on with the show. Sadly, during the next two hours only about three people showed up and one bought a book.

I was sweating profusely for the entire two hours. Thoughts of getting fired and looking for another job kept creeping into my mind. Fortunately for me, the author and her husband were wonderful about everything. They took it all with a grain of salt, reassuring me over and over that these sorts of things happen during author tours and I did not have a thing to worry about. This being my first author tour, I hoped what they were telling me was true. Regardless, it was a long drive home.

Well, their words turned out to be true. Had they not, I probably wouldn't have spent the past twenty-five years working in the publishing industry. Certainly I would not be writing these words today. Because that author was my first experience, her kindness and thoughtfulness helped me make a connection with the business. Her name was Patricia Matthews, a romance writer; her husband was Clayton. I will never forget their kindness.

Remembering how they treated me at such an early stage in my career gives me hope that there are many well-deserving writers out there who could use a little help from me in getting their career off to a good start. I hope this writing will help them work within the system to get their books published successfully.

So, to all writers who want to get their work published successfully, these words are for you. Because after twenty-five years of working inside the business of publishing, it is time I work from the outside to help you become successful.

For me, now, it is all about the writers and the books.

About the Author

Jerry's career in publishing began in the fall of 1977 as a Sales Representative for Ballantine Books, a division of Random House. In 1979 he joined the book division of Independent News, one of the distribution groups at Warner Communications, where he spent more than twenty-three years in sales and management. During that time the company expanded to become The Time Warner Book Group.

Jerry's sales team distributed over a thousand titles a year from a number of large publishing houses and imprints, including Little, Brown; Warner Books and Hyperion. He retired as Vice-President, Director of Field Sales in 2003.

Jerry is the founder of www.WritersReaders.com —the informational website for writers—and the creator of TIPS for WRITERS, a Newsletter of valuable information for writers.

He is also the founder of www.NothingBinding.com, the community for writers and authors of independently published books.

Now Jerry spends his time writing, teaching and speaking with writers about the importance of understanding the marketplace for selling books and the business of publishing.

About the Editor

Nancy McCurry is a freelance editor and operates *All About Books*, a Phoenix-based editing bureau. She received her BA from Vermont College and her Master of Fine Arts in writing from Goddard College. Nancy is a writing teacher, has published in fiction and nonfiction and been granted both national and academic awards.

All About Books offers various editing services, consultation, workshops and resources to assist writers throughout the creative process. www.NancyMcCurry.com.

Dear Writer,

Thank you for your purchase of this book. I hope you find it helpful and informative.

Please take a moment to visit my website, www.WritersReaders.com, and fill out a short survey about the purchase of this book. Click on the About Jerry page and answer the questions in the column on the right. Your feedback helps us provide the products and services you want.

My website, www.WritersReaders.com, is committed to providing the tools necessary to help writers become successfully published authors.

For a complete list of all products and services, visit www.WritersReaders.com and click on the Books & More page. Sign up for the free Newsletter, TIPS for WRITERS, which provides valuable information about the business of publishing.

Finally, please take a moment to browse the Independent Writers of www.NothingBinding.com, where you are welcome to profile your own writing and yourself as part of our growing community, and where voices never heard and stories never told are offered to readers around the world.

Thank you,

Jerry D. Simmons